Victorian Classics

of San Francisco

Design: Wayne and Linda Bonnett
Editor: Wayne Bonnett
Copy Editor: Marian G. Witwer
Typography: Rippens & Tate
Printing: Tien Wah Press (Pte) Ltd. Singapore
Co-ordinated by: Palace Press

Library of Congress Cataloging-in-Publication Data

Victorian Classics of San Francisco.

   Includes index.
   1. Architecture, Domestic--California--San Francisco
--Pictorial works. 2. Architecture, Victorian--
California--San Francisco--Pictorial works.
3. Architecture, Modern--19th century--San Francisco--
Pictorial works. 4. San Francisco (Calif.)--Buildings,
structures, etc.--Pictorial works.

NA7238.S35V5 1987   728.3′7′0979461   86-32553
ISBN 0-915269-05-8

Windgate Press
P.O.Box 1715 Sausalito, California 94966

FIRST EDITION

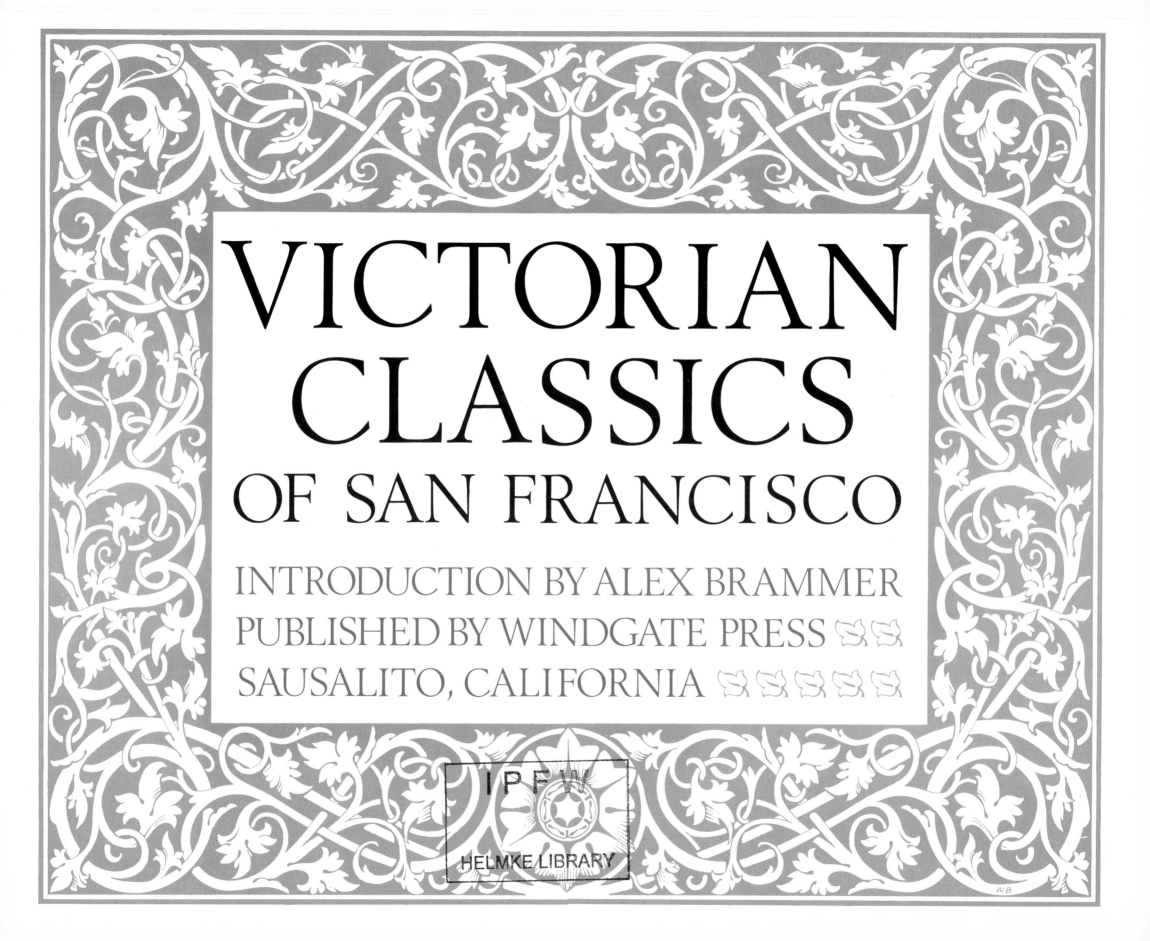

VICTORIAN CLASSICS
OF SAN FRANCISCO

INTRODUCTION BY ALEX BRAMMER
PUBLISHED BY WINDGATE PRESS
SAUSALITO, CALIFORNIA

(From the *San Francisco Newsletter*, June 23, 1888)

⊰AN ÷ ALBUM⊱

Artistic Homes of California

We are now preparing an Album of the "Artistic Homes of California," which we intend making the most elaborate publication ever issued on the Pacific Coast. It will contain Fifty Illustrations of the Handsomest Residences in San Francisco, Oakland and San Jose, beautifully printed by the new Artotype process, which we have now brought to such perfection that the softness of tone in the reproduction far surpasses the original photograph.

There will be a graphic description of each Illustration, printed in clear, new type, on eighty-pound plate paper. The Album will be elegantly bound in heavy Covers, and will prove a most valuable and attractive addition to the library, parlor, drawing room or reading room, or wherever "we most do congregate," and will possess the advantage of giving a concise and pleasing idea of San Francisco and vicinity.

Every person with California's interest at heart should feel a pride in sending this Album to friends abroad, and thus showing the refinement and elegance of our Homes.

Visitors and Tourists will obtain a clearer conception of San Francisco, and secure the most pleasing reminder of their visit by securing this Album.

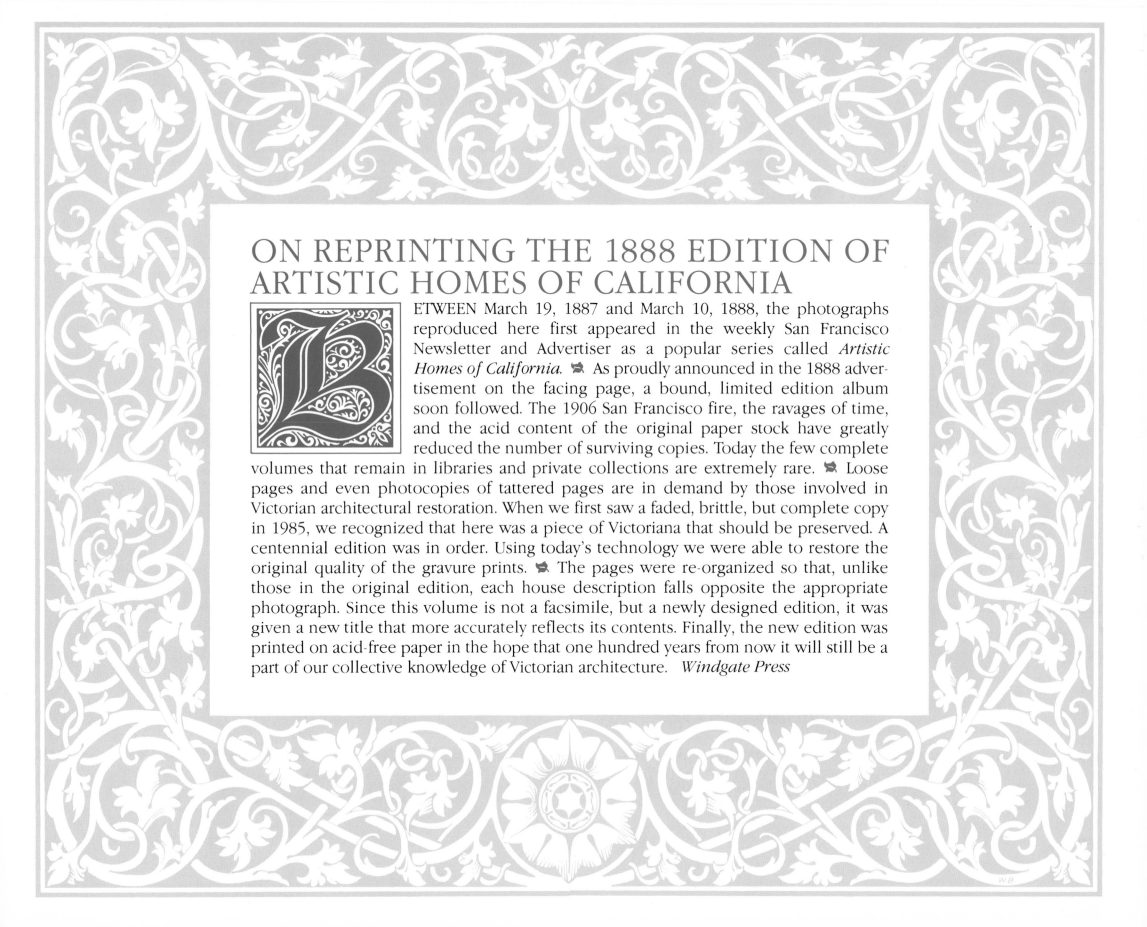

ON REPRINTING THE 1888 EDITION OF ARTISTIC HOMES OF CALIFORNIA

ETWEEN March 19, 1887 and March 10, 1888, the photographs reproduced here first appeared in the weekly San Francisco Newsletter and Advertiser as a popular series called *Artistic Homes of California.* 🐌 As proudly announced in the 1888 advertisement on the facing page, a bound, limited edition album soon followed. The 1906 San Francisco fire, the ravages of time, and the acid content of the original paper stock have greatly reduced the number of surviving copies. Today the few complete volumes that remain in libraries and private collections are extremely rare. 🐌 Loose pages and even photocopies of tattered pages are in demand by those involved in Victorian architectural restoration. When we first saw a faded, brittle, but complete copy in 1985, we recognized that here was a piece of Victoriana that should be preserved. A centennial edition was in order. Using today's technology we were able to restore the original quality of the gravure prints. 🐌 The pages were re-organized so that, unlike those in the original edition, each house description falls opposite the appropriate photograph. Since this volume is not a facsimile, but a newly designed edition, it was given a new title that more accurately reflects its contents. Finally, the new edition was printed on acid-free paper in the hope that one hundred years from now it will still be a part of our collective knowledge of Victorian architecture. *Windgate Press*

INTRODUCTION

VICTORIAN SAN FRANCISCO is a phrase that conjures up a romantic past, a past filled with images of nineteenth century America. While San Francisco today has a high-rise skyline and all the other mixed blessings that help define a modern city, San Francisco of the imagination is a Victorian city of gas-lit cobblestone streets, clanging cable cars, a boisterous, vital waterfront crowded with sailing ships, and Nob Hill, crowned with fabulous mansions of the Comstock silver kings and railroad barons. Although relatively little of that San Francisco remains today, the City is nonetheless perceived as being not only rooted in the Victorian period, but also strongly protective of its nineteenth century heritage.

San Francisco was perhaps the last Victorian city. In the early 1850s when English and eastern American cities already reflected the architectural and social peculiarities that we now identify as Victorian, San Francisco was a disorganized collection of tents and plank shacks. San Francisco as a city came into being, endured a lengthy adolescence, and reached maturity all within the reign of Queen Victoria. And most of that city perished in the 1906 holocaust, just five years after the death of Victoria.

From the Gold Rush years of the 1850s to the time of Queen Victoria's death in 1901, San Francisco had blossomed into the preeminent city of the American West Coast. The City had a polished exterior (facade, some might call it) of Victorian splendor, covering the rough, innovative, opportunistic soul of the American frontier. In less than thirty years San Francisco rose from village to metropolis. Between the 1870s when the famous Nob Hill mansions adorned that former sand hill and the 1880s when Van Ness Avenue became the home of the mercantile moguls, the City produced a spectacular display of residential architecture never since equalled. Money, transport and merchandising all centered in San Francisco, and the very spirit of American optimism and enterprise radiated from it. It was only fitting that the movers and shakers of San Francisco should have homes that radiated success and prosperity.

A prospect of unlimited growth stretched before San Francisco, and it became almost a civic duty for its wealthy citizens to build not only massive business blocks and hotels bearing their names, but great mansions as well. These homes were the embodiment of wealth and success in Victorian San Francisco. They were the pride of an entire generation of San Franciscans. In suburban towns on the San Francisco Peninsula, and in the nearby cities of Oakland and San Jose, large and stylish homes were constructed that equaled, if not exceeded, the grandeur of those in San Francisco.

The homes of the growing middle class also reflected the pattern set by the mansions. Here were columned front porches, romantic towers, 16 foot high ceilings, jeweled and

Two of the finer examples of Victorian architecture to grace San Francisco's fashionable Van Ness Avenue in the 1880's were the Ashe mansion on the Southwest corner of Van Ness Avenue and Washington Street (on the left), and the residence of Mr. Charles Holbrook (on the right).

stained glass in profusion, and an incredible array of wooden filigree. Stretching block upon block, these wooden creations that even in an era of splendid rococo architecture were noted for their exuberance exactly suited the mood of San Francisco.

This inordinate civic pride often blossomed forth in the local press. "The people of our great Eastern cities, and still more those of the older communities of Europe, will doubtless find it hard to believe that here, in far-off California, we have some of the most magnificent specimens of architecture to be seen in either hemisphere. Such, however, is the case. Taken either in detail or as a whole, it is the opinion of artists, critics, and cultured travelers generally who have seen them that the homes of our leading citizens here on Nob Hill are works unexcelled in the world." The early San Francisco press was enthusiastic, although not particularly known for its modesty.

Among the numerous early newspapers was a relatively sedate weekly tabloid called the *San Francisco Newsletter and California Special Circular.* Launched in July, 1856, the *San Francisco Newsletter* prospered as a newsy, gossipy six-page publication throughout San Francisco's turbulent adolescence. In the late 1880s the *San Francisco Newsletter and California Advertiser,* as it was now called, introduced photographs to its pages. At first the photos were prints of famous paintings and lithographs reproduced by gravure and inserted in the newsletter. These "Artotypes" struck the fancy of the citizenry and were collected by readers. In the March 19, 1887, issue a series of artotypes was begun, called "Artistic Homes of California." No doubt the title was inspired by *Artistic Homes of New York,* a book published shortly before in New York. "Artistic" had replaced the shopworn "elegant" in Victorian society, and was the ultimate adjective applied to domestic architecture and interior fashions. The *San Francisco Newsletter*'s series was immensely popular from its inception. Although at first the homes illustrated were limited to those in San Francisco, the series eventually included examples from San Jose and Oakland.

Each week a local photographer would make an 8 by 10 inch glass plate negative of the subject house (there must have been fierce competition to have one's home included in the series), then the San Francisco firm of Britton and Rey would make a gravure plate or "artotype" from the negative and run off a sufficient number of prints for inclusion in the next edition. If the photograph didn't turn out, a substitute "art print" of a Rembrandt painting or a Civil War battle panorama would appear in that week's *Newsletter.* On one occasion this was explained, not very convincingly, as follows: "Aiming, as we do, to attain perfection in every detail of this collection, we this week present a stirring scene, the Assault on Vicksburg. There are some six or seven of these panoramas now on exhibition in this country, and we expect, from time to time, to scatter views from them among the 'Artistic Homes.'"

By the fifth week readers were clamoring for more than just formal portraits of the houses. The editors were proud to announce in the April 16, 1887, issue that henceforth the *Newsletter* would include a condensed description of the interiors of each house, "so universal has been the desire to know more about these residences than could possibly be portrayed in a photograph."

It was soon announced that a bound volume of the artotypes and their accompanying descriptions would be produced by the *Newsletter.* The editors confidently stated their intent to make it "the most elaborate publication ever issued on the Pacific Coast." While the album may not have quite lived up to that expectation, it was very handsome indeed and became a coveted possession that would be held by families and collectors for generations. The *Newsletter* went on to produce a second series, which included civic and commercial buildings in San Francisco. The second bound volume, also called *Artistic Homes of California,* was issued in 1891 and was not as popular as the first. By that time, San Francisco domestic architecture had been featured in many publications and the series was not unique, as the first had been.

Like the classic Victorian homes in the photographs, many copies of *Artistic Homes of California* went up in flames in the 1906 San Francisco conflagration. The original photographs and gravure plates were destroyed with the *Newsletter* offices on Bush Street. Surviving copies of *Artistic Homes of California* became even more scarce, until today they are rare to the point of unavailability.

This volume is a reconstruction of the original first edition of *Artistic Homes of California*. Here are the most aspired to, copied, and discussed homes in the state prior to 1900. San Franciscans, like most Americans after the Civil War, had been dazzled by the opportunities afforded builders and architects by the introduction of mass-production methods. Wooden and metal filigree, ornate plaster and concrete castings, embossed tin and leather, and encaustic tiles all provided architects a limitless variety of visual effects for interiors and exteriors. Plentiful redwood lumber locally available plus the demands of the period for display guaranteed that the results would be spectacular. What developed was a rich and diverse architecture which even the strictest critics could never say was dull.

Although now collectively called "Victorian," the houses in this volume include several distinct styles. They can be identified as "Italianate," "Mansard," "Stick," "Queen Anne," "Romanesque," and "Colonial Revival." The styles came into fashion at about five-year intervals, beginning in 1870. As each new style emerged and was quickly copied, it was almost universally praised at the time for its elegance and beauty. However, now and again an ugly criticism would appear. "Mr. Charles Crocker" says the *Telegraph* "has purchased a handsome residence in New York. He deserves the very handsomest residence in America for the patience and truly Christian fortitude with which he has long endured the most hideous. There are uglier buildings in America than the Crocker house on Nob Hill (Plate 6), but they were built with public money for a public purpose; among the architectural triumphs of private fortune and personal taste it is peerless. If Mr. Crocker doesn't want it anymore, I'd like to burn it down." Such stinging criticism was, however, considered no more than sour grapes by most observers. It is safe to say that these same observers would have been awestruck to realize that most of these houses were destined to vanish soon in flames. It is fortunate that "Artistic Homes of California" had captured them forever in their glory.

Although the photos and accompanying descriptions of interiors vividly illustrate the houses themselves, they give little hint of the lives that were led in these grand mansions. Yet each house does have its tale to tell, though sometimes the memories have dimmed with the passage of time.

Genevieve Bothin de Limur would tell her grandchildren how the family home was dynamited to break the progress of the 1906 fire and how she had used the occasion to get rid of a hated black dress by leaving it behind in the doomed house. Her cousin Donald Maas remembered happier times at the Bothin mansion (Plate 34), such as the formal Sunday luncheons with a footman standing behind each dining room chair. One woman who was a child during that distant era fondly remembers the white porcelain cuspidors that stood on each side of the mantle in the front parlor. She says, "It is surprising that no daring mind ever was tempted to establish the utility of the two little squatting guards, but throughout twenty years of Thursdays-at-Home, no one ever did, and when the great earthquake closed that chapter of their uneventful lives, it was as unsullied virgins that they mounted into flame."

Each of the fifty "Artistic Homes," whether in San Francisco, Oakland, or San Jose, was considered important in its day. Most were included because of their architectural distinction, some for the prominence of their owners. Houses that changed hands during their glory days often became identified with subsequent owners rather than the original ones.

Built by Edwin Crocker as a wedding gift shortly after the 1882 marriage of his daughter Aimee Crocker to R. Porter Ashe, the mansion included this grand oak and walnut lined entrance hall (described in the text accompanying Plate 1). The interiors of the "Artistic Homes" were finished with as much richness and attention to detail as the exteriors.

One such example is the mansion illustrated in Plate One: the R. Porter Ashe residence. It was later known as the Hobart residence, and even as the City of Paris department store. It was one of the most glamorous residences in San Francisco, and now one of the least remembered. The house was built by Judge and Mrs. Edwin B. Crocker of Sacramento as a bridal gift for their beautiful daughter Aimee, when her marriage in December, 1882 to Mr. Porter Ashe became an acknowledged fact.

Aimee was an uninhibited spirit whose sensational escapades were shockers in her day. Even the circumstances of her first marriage, when she was in her teens, are highly entertaining. The story goes that R. Porter Ashe and William Wallace, both prominent lawyers, shook dice for the lady's hand. Wallace won. The bridal party departed by train from Sacramento for San Francisco, where the ceremony was to take place. *En route,* Wallace left the coach for the smoking car. Ashe, also on board, saw his opportunity, seized it, and persuaded Aimee to get off the train and marry him in Martinez, a little town 30 miles east of San Francisco.

At first Aimee's mother refused to recognize the marriage, but after a few unhappy weeks she relented. Loving letters were exchanged, and the bride and bridegroom were pardoned. The mansion on Van Ness Avenue was their gift.

There was a story that Aimee arrived at the construction site one day in carriage-and-pair and asked for the architect and contractor. To them she expressed her desire for a small swimming pool or "plunge bath," as it was then called.

"We had better excavate about there," said the contractor, indicating with his hand, "if you want a bath to swim in."

"No, sir," she replied after a thought or two, and looking the architect squarely in the eyes, "I want it on the *top* floor."

The architect never batted an eye, but said: "You can have it suspended *above* the roof, if your father says he'll pay for it."

It was built on the top floor as she wished.

Aimee's husband had been born of a traditional American family of some import in the American colonies and in post-revolutionary American government. R. Porter Ashe followed brilliantly in the footsteps of his forefathers who had given their name to Asheville, North Carolina.

Ashe was a sportsman. Wherever race horses ran and pugilists fought, there Ashe could be found. His stable held some of the finest horses on the American tracks. In San Francisco society and its club world, R. Porter Ashe's name was well-known. In those cotillion days he and a small Nob Hill coterie dictated the ways of the social elite.

In time, the fame of R. Porter Ashe as a host became worldwide, and the home on Washington Street was a mecca for many visiting celebrities. His friendships with Lily Langtry and Lotta Crabtree were the source of much gossip.

Aimee's escapades in the mansion are also well documented. One neighbor remembered seeing her at an early morning hour in full evening regalia driving a garbage cart home from a party. Another recalled strolling past the house one night and seeing Aimee through the open drawing room windows sitting atop the grand piano playing the keys with her bare feet. It is said that at a party she gave honoring Oscar Wilde, Aimee drank him under the table.

Mr. and Mrs. Ashe were divorced, surprising no one, and Aimee went on to have four husbands and many romances. Her last husband was Prince Galitzin of Russia who was 26 years old to her 62. Soon after her divorce from Ashe the mansion had been sold to Walter Scott Hobart, a well known millionaire mine owner. His daughters the Misses Alice and Ella Hobart were leaders of the *beau monde* in the 1890s and early 1900s, and the mansion continued as one of the centers of the fashionable world. Ella Hobart also became a Russian Princess by marrying Prince Zourab Tchkotoua.

The Hobarts hastily moved from the mansion on April 19, 1906, as the great fire moved closer to Van Ness Avenue. But the house survived, although it never again served as a residence. It was remodelled as the temporary quarters for the City of Paris department store, which had been burned out of

Even as it fell to the wreckers in 1913, the Ashe mansion maintained its stoic dignity. The ornate interiors are being dismantled and the pieces stacked along Van Ness Avenue.

its downtown location. "It was a curious experience", wrote Amelia Ransome Neville, "to enter a store by a marble vestibule, find yourself in a beautiful great hall with carved oak staircase and stained glass windows, to have the goods you desired brought to you from the pantry or sideboard drawers or from the library shelves, to have them spread before you on a great dining table . . . or in another room, to be served at a hastily improvised pine counter. If you wandered up the stairway to look at suits or coats, perhaps you were asked to step into the bathroom to be fitted."

In 1913, no longer needed as a house or a business, the mansion was demolished to make way for the building that presently stands on the site. Van Ness Avenue would never again be the grand residential street it had once been.

The earthquake and fire of 1906 marked the turning point in the fortunes of the "Artistic Homes." In four terrible days in April their era of magnificence ended. The flames swept up and over Nob Hill leveling everything except the stone outer walls of the Flood mansion and the shell of the new Fairmont Hotel. Van Ness Avenue marked the western fire line, and in trying to contain the conflagration it was decided to destroy all the buildings on the east side of the street.

Years later, Olive Holbrook Palmer described the ghastly scene. "At the time of the fire they dynamited all the homes on the east side of the avenue to save the buildings on [the west] side. The Government men ordered us out of the house (Plate 4) and we left thinking that our home was going to be destroyed too. We stood on Franklin Street and watched the houses being blown up, the homes of our friends.

"And it was a strange thing—the way those houses fell. You'd expect that the explosion would throw debris high into the air," she said, "but it wasn't like that at all. The big houses simply folded in on themselves and crumpled. The debris didn't even reach the sidewalk."

The big homes that survived in San Francisco and the bay area would fall victim to changing tastes and changing neighborhoods. New critics would write of the Victorian palaces, "The man who made a sudden fortune was apt to think that nothing was good in architecture except the ornate. As a consequence he built a great wooden barn and covered it with all the 'gingerbread' decorations the planing mills could provide, then called his misshapen home a masterpiece of art and a palace."

Over the next 50 years, time was not kind to the survivors, and progress would decree "down with the old and up with the new." So, one by one, the great Victorian mansions were replaced by apartment houses or commercial buildings. "Sixty Years Of San Francisco History End In A Used Car Lot" the headline reads as the Holbrook home faced the wrecker's ball in 1946.

The William Martin home (Plate 32) was used as a back drop in a feature film shortly before its demolition in the early 1950s. Bits and pieces of dissected interiors turned up as props in other movies and also as parts of other houses. By the 1960s only a handful of the original "Artistic Homes" remained (such as the Haas, Stone and Payne mansions). As the number of survivors dwindled, Victorian architecture of all stripes and styles was "rediscovered" and enjoyed a resurgence of popularity that continues today.

One hundred years after the photographs in this album were made, the memory of the grand homes remains a part of the lore of San Francisco and the Bay Area. For later generations, born long after the Golden Age recalled in these photos, fascination with Victorian architecture is stronger than ever. We take pride in the few remaining "Artistic Homes," and many carefully restored and lovingly maintained Victorian houses attest to our renewed interest. Through the photos and descriptions presented here we can indulge our fascination and let our imaginations take us back to another time.

Alex Brammer
San Francisco, 1987

TABLE of ARTOTYPES

ARTISTIC HOMES OF CALIFORNIA

San Francisco is not the city of sand hills, or the collection of cloth and paper houses, once it was, but a growing metropolis, in which wealth, culture and refinement have a habitation and a home. Nor are the buildings a senseless repetition of each other. A marked, distinctive individuality has left its influence on most of these artistic homes, and though certain characteristic features unavoidably are reproduced, they have been so modified by the exercise of individual taste and judgment that a striking variety is the result. In this album are houses representing almost every stage in the city's growth—from the Italian order of architecture, with its porticoes, which prevailed in the 1850's, up through the mansard roof and cupola period, to the style of the French Renaissance, the Queen Anne and Colonial style, and all the varied forms of the modern Gothic. It might not be without interest to trace the evolution of the domestic order of architecture from the square four walled house, the inevitable bow window, and the stiff front stoop with its railed balcony above. The corner tower, with its grand possibilities for swell bays; the picturesque gables and their loggias; the artistic roofs, with their decks and towers between the gables; the great sheets of window glass, have all lent their aid to the improvement of our present houses. It would be difficult to classify these residences as belonging to any one style of architecture, for all the different orders have been reproduced, either entirely or partially, with what may be termed a free treatment. Not only by the grace and beauty, or by the uniqueness of their exterior, have these residences called forth admiration, but what must impress a dweller in the crowded cities in the East and of Europe, is that the houses—are surrounded by spacious grounds, extensive lawns and gardens, in a high state of cultivation,—and all this is a city.

But, artistic, attractive, or stately, noble and imposing as many of the residences are in the exterior, the interiors have been constructed with a view to comfort and convenience, combined with much elegance and architectural beauty. The picturesque shape of the exterior gives to the interior many pleasing irregularities of shape, which are taken advantage of principally by window effects with broad window seats. In many of our homes, besides the two parlors, with their folding doors, or the double room, with its broad arch, the entire floor may be thrown en suite, making one vast and varied apartment. The hall has expanded into an imposing entrance of vestibule, entrance hall, main hall and staircase hall, with a profusion of art glass windows. The woodwork has risen from an imitated splendor to the glory of the genuine wood, wrought into panels and carvings, and polished with marvelous beauty.

The white marble mantel has given place to the mantel of carved wood or of California onyx, with its elaborate chimneypiece of shelves and beveled mirrors; the fireplace is tiled with the triumphs of baked and painted clay; the staring white walls and the florid frescoes have yielded to the tints, the friezes, and the borders, and the lincrusta effects now in vogue; and instead of the stationary washstand in the bedroom—once the acme of a handsome house—all the bed chambers have dressing rooms attached. As to the conveniences and household appliances, they are beyond enumeration.

In conclusion, while it must be admitted that the system of architecture is latitudinarian, it may be asked whether any other would better correspond with the requirements of people in this climate, so fortunately exempt from the extremes of heat and cold. The question of site, perspective and general conformity to the outline of the location on which a house is to be built, is coming to be more and more considered. The tendency of builders is to embellish without sacrificing convenience, to unite simplicity with richness, and to suppress innovations that may lead to gaudiness. This is the triumph of art.

RESIDENCE OF MR. R. PORTER ASHE

MAGNIFICENT in its proportions, impressive in its architecture and harmonious in every detail, this residence on Van Ness Avenue and Washington Street cannot be adequately described in the brief space allotted to it. A flight of massive granite steps mount to the marble porch before the double entrance doors of solid oak, which roll back, disclosing a vestibule, tiled in colors, with mahogany dado, and frescoed walls and ceiling. The vestibule doors are enriched with jeweled art glass, and open into the spacious entrance hall, which, spanned by an arch, narrows into the main hall that, terminating with another arch, leads to the grand staircase hall beyond. From the entrance, the flight with the rich art glass window, representing a battle scene, set above the landing, from which two reverse lateral branches mount to the second floor, is plainly visible.

All the floors of the first story are oak inlaid with walnut in border designs. The halls and grand staircase are finished in oak. In the entrance hall the dado is very high, each panel being surmounted by a square with armorial bearings. The ceiling is also of oak, squared by transverse moldings. On the right of the entrance hall is the reception room finished in white and gold, the walls tinted in French gray. In the north, recessed within a square bay window, is a mantel of California onyx, surmounted by a mirror in frame of bronze relief. Beyond this apartment and opening into the main hall is the parlor, or from its characteristic features, the Turkish room. It is finished in Oriental style, the sidewalls have the effect of burnished metal, and the ceiling is frescoed with sunbursts. The upholstery is all of an Eastern design; the ornaments, the unique fireplace and chimneypiece in the west all correspond with the one idea. On each side of the fireplace a door admits to the billiard room, which is also entered from the staircase hall where the walls and ceiling are resplendent with embossed lincrusta in colors. The woodwork including a high paneled dado is of satin finished redwood. The chimneypiece on the east surmounts a fireplace set in blue tiles.

On the left of the entrance hall, directly opposite the reception room is the library finished in black walnut, heavily carved and highly polished with panels of brass relief and frescoed ceiling. The mantel and fireplace are set in the south. Beyond the library, and also entered from the main hall, is the dining room, finished in mahogany. Communicating with both library dining room, is a cozy little breakfast room finished in ash. A magnificent buffet occupies a large portion of the western wall; to its right is a large stained glass window with window seat. In the south is the fireplace set in pressed brick, and ornamented with glazed tiles. The chimneypiece projects forward with a hooded top, and in either side of the fireplace, under the shelter of the chimneypiece, are seats in the "inglenook." From the dining room, at the left of the fireplace, and the rear hall, which is of considerable length, terminating at its further end at the smoking room. From it descent is made to the basement with its kitchen, laundry, storerooms, servants' dining room and furnace room. In the rear hall is also an elevator, clothes chute and dust chute.

In the second story the staircase is surmounted by arcaded walls, which frescoed and ornate with gilding, render the staircase still more impressive. The two principal chambers front upon Van Ness Avenue. There are three large spare rooms—besides the nursery, sewing room and linen room. To the chambers dressing rooms are attached.

BRITTON & REY, ARTO.

PLATE 1

Van Ness Avenue & Washington Street, San Francisco

Curlett & Cuthbertson, Architects

Residence of Mr. Theodore F. Payne

ENTIRELY unlike any other house in the city, is this residence on the south side of Sutter Street, between Franklin and Gough. The artotype gives a very good view of the exterior with its numerous bay windows, the tower and its loggia, the ivy grown colonial chimney and the extensive *porte cochere*. A flight of stone steps mount to the entrance, the doors of which are solid oak, heavily paneled. These open into a small oak walled vestibule with an inlaid floor.

The reception room embracing the swell window on the northwest corner of the house. This is elegantly finished in oak, lincrusta, and tinted walls. It also opens into the grand hall which extends beyond the vestibule. On the left of the vestibule, and also on the left of the main hall is the parlor. This is a spacious apartment which on its southwest corner includes the round window of the tower elevation, thus adding greatly to the appearance and extent of the room. Its sidewalls are delicately tinted in French gray, and the ceiling is frescoed, with effective cornice. The mantel and chimneypiece are of ebony, the fireplace is set in dark tiling and the woodwork is of cocobola and ebony. Beyond is the library, tinted, and finished in oak. Still further beyond is the dining room, finished in antique oak, and possessing a charming southeastern exposure. Connected with the dining room are the butler's pantry, lavatory, rear hall and stairs and kitchen. On this side also is the carriage entrance.

The grand hall into which the vestibule and all these apartments open directly, or communicate by means of a branch hall, is nearly square, with inlaid floor, tinted in Pompeiian red, and finished in oak. The ceiling is barred off by transverse moldings. By an admirable arrangement of windows, art glass and plate, the hall is excellently lighted. The staircase rises in the southern portion of the hall, mounts toward the east and turns again to reach the second story. The principal chamber is over the parlor. In all, including guest chambers, nursery, sewing room and servants' rooms, there are twelve apartments above the first floor; some of them having dressing rooms attached. The house is furnished elegantly, the portieres are particularly rich, and the woodwork is exquisitely finished. In the basement are the laundry, wine cellar, furnace room and storerooms.

1409 Sutter Street, San Francisco

Curlett & Cuthbertson, Architects

Plate 2

Residence of Mr. R. H. Pease, Jr.

NO more comprehensive prospect of San Francisco Bay and its environs is possessed by any other residences in San Francisco, than is spread out below the windows of this elegant residence on the northwest corner of Pacific Avenue and Pierce Street. Its exterior is faithfully represented by one of the best executed artotypes in the entire series. Its interior, as regards the finishing, furnishing, the completeness of all its appointments, and the atmosphere of combined comfort, taste and elegance, is not to be surpassed. The service is electric, and the windows remarkable for the unbroken extent of their view.

The double entrance doors of the porch fold back into the vestibule. The doors of solid Spanish cedar, lighted by art glass, open directly into the hall, which is floored with ash and finished in redwood, as are all the rooms on this floor. The sidewalls are tinted in terra-cotta, with dado of the same color in lincrusta, illustrating a Moorish design. The ceiling is curly redwood, crossbarred.

On the right of the hall is the parlor in dark cardinal, with another Moorish pattern expressed in the dado. The southeast corner is enclosed in two large windows at right angles with a broad window seat. In the northeast corner is a beautiful mantel and chimneypiece of cocobola wood, and the fireplace set in tiles. On the north opening out of the parlor is the library which expands into the hall on the west, with no intervening wall between. It is finished like the hall. The open fireplace, on the north, with its chimneypiece of Spanish cedar, the staircase on the west, with a wide conservatory window under the flight, and the angular bay window, on the east, with cut glass ornamentation, all combine to render the library exceedingly picturesque. Still further to the north is the dining room, a bright cheery apartment, with pressed brick fireplace, and mahogany mantel and chimneypiece.

The window looking toward the north has an uninterrupted view across to Sausalito, the Coast Range, Berkeley, Oakland and Alameda. The Moorish dado is surmounted by the turquoise blue on the sidewalls and ceilings. From the dining room and also from the back hall, which with its attendant features of rear stairs and lavatory in shut off from the front hall, may be approached the billiard room. The dado is ornamental design. The walls and ceiling are papered. The mantel is of walnut with glazed brick fireplace, and there are several windows in effective positions. In the basement are the kitchen, laundry, storerooms and wine cellar. In the second story are six chambers connected by dressing rooms. There are cedar closets and linen room. In the attic are four bedrooms, the servants' apartments, and large storeroom. There is a side entrance on the west.

Pacific Avenue & Pierce Street, San Francisco

Clinton Day, Architect

PLATE 3

Residence of Mr. Charles Holbrook

GABLES and tower, turrets, loggias, bay windows and Gothic porch combine to make this residence on the northwest corner of Van Ness Avenue and Washington Street one of the most picturesque and attractive in the series. It is approached by an impressive flight of granite steps which rises to the platform before the double entrance doors opening upon the tile paved vestibule. The vestibule doors with their art glass sashes open into the main hall which extends through the center of the house—that is, from east to west. It is finished in black walnut and terminates at the door which shuts off communication with the rear hall, and also at the foot of the walnut staircase. This mounts towards the west, at half the height between the first and second story. It is broken by a landing, from which the staircase makes a reverse turn, ascending to the upper floor. The two halls are lighted by a domed skylight which rests upon Corinthian columns partially set in the four walls. The effect is very fine.

On the right of the main hall is the parlor with black walnut mantel on the north; and fireplace set in old gold and bronze tiles; the whole surmounted by a large square beveled plate mirror. Over the square bay window in the east, and over all the window sashes as well on this floor, are jeweled art glass lights. On the left of the hall is the library also in black walnut with the southeast corner of the room expanded in a square bay window. On the south is an elaborate walnut mantel. Beyond is the dining room finished in oak.

In the south is a large square window used as a conservatory, with tiled floor, and filled with plants. A door in the west wall opens into the butler's pantry, rear hall and kitchen. On the north, another door opens into the rear hall, stairs and closets. From the rear hall a door opens upon a flight of stairs descending to the basement, in which are the billiard room, furnace room, wine cellar and storerooms. In the second floor the principal suite is over the library and dining room with dressing room between. Over the parlor is another fine chamber. Besides these there are two other sleeping apartments, bathrooms, linen closet and sewing room. In the third story are the servants' apartments, spare rooms, bath and trunk rooms. The service is electric.

Plate 4

Van Ness Avenue & Washington Street, San Francisco

A. C. Macy, Architect

Residence of Mr. William Dunphy

CROWNING the highest point in the city, and plainly discernible from Golden Gate Park, this beautiful residence, on Washington Street between Gough and Octavia, has an unequaled view which nothing can ever abbreviate. The grounds in front are devoted to lawns and flowers, while in the rear the grassy slope is terraced down to Jackson Street, where a tall wire fence keeps the deer within the deer park. The approach to the house is paved with white and black marble in geometrical design. The entrance is guarded by double doors of mahogany, and a stained glass representation of Tasso and his pupils. The hall, long and wide, extends through the center of the house and terminates at the sitting room door. The floor is inlaid with maple and oak, with mahogany and jeweled lincrusta-walton dado. The chandelier, depending from the frescoed ceiling, is of an oriental design in gold bronze and jewels. Massive mahogany doors open from the left side of the hall into the parlor, a room of impressive dimensions; carpeted with a product of the famous Gobelin loom. It is frescoed beautifully; with cut glass chandeliers and mirrors. At the lower end of the parlor, on either side of the door, is a niche, hung with blue plush as a background, for white marble statues upon their pedestals of onyx.

Opening from the parlor is the library, a room octagonal in shape, being the first story of the tower at the northwest corner of the building. It is filled with books, the ceiling frescoed, the walls of quiet color, the inlaid floor of maple, oak and walnut, covered with Turkish rugs. The atmosphere is suggestive of that calm and seclusion so dear to the heart of a student. The library also opens into the main hall. A look into the sitting room close by discloses a pleasant home-like apartment.

On the right of the main hall the first door opens into the music room, hung with oriental curtains, and furnished in oriental style. At the right hang the Japanese bead curtains, which swing and sway back into place with a sweet sound. Beyond them is the tiled conservatory, which connects with the dining room, full of the morning sunlight. Its floor is inlaid with walnut and oak; the dado is paneled black walnut, and the frieze is lincrusta-walton in fruit design; the ceiling is frescoed. Massive double doors open out into the main hall, and beyond them, at right angles to the hall, the mahogany staircase ascends to the second floor, on which are the family apartments. In the third story is a grand skylight of ground and etched glass, and the large ballroom, which is tinted in lavendar. The billiard room has recently been built in the basement. Leading from the ballroom is the observatory in the tower, which, in its turn, is surmounted by a smaller room, also used as an observatory.

2122 Washington Street, San Francisco

B. MacDougall & Son, Architects

PLATE 5

Residence of Mr. Charles Crocker

APART from the great size of this building, which was erected on the northwest corner of California and Taylor Streets in 1877, there is much in its architectural features to entitle it to particular consideration. It is built in the style of the French Renaissance, a style which permits an ornate elaboration of detail, of which privilege the architects were not slow to take advantage. The front entrance, approached from California Street, is reached by a wide and impressive staircase of granite. The main structure is of wood, while the basement walls are of solid masonry. Many artistic details are introduced into the facade, relieving whatever is heavy in design or construction; so that, considering its size, the edifice is regarded as one of the most beautiful architectural masterpieces to be found in any State in the Union.

The interior is distinguished by a perfect arrangement of the halls and rooms, and by the high studding of each story. The main hall leads immediately from the vestibule to a cross hall, which is nearly in the center of the building. The wood work is mahogany. Opening at the right of main hall is the library, a large room, containing several graceful irregularities, and on the left is the drawing room, similar in form and dimensions, each richly frescoed, with elegant cornices, grand chandeliers and other ornamental features. Leading from the library is Mrs. Crocker's boudoir, behind it is the principal chamber, bathroom and dressing room. Still further behind these is the main dining hall, and in close proximity to it are the butler's pantry and other similar rooms. These are all on the Taylor Street side. In the rear of the drawing room and connecting with it, on the left of the hall, is the art gallery, and adjoining it is the circular statuary gallery. Back of the art gallery, and entered from it or from the hall, is the billiard room. Directly opposite the main entrance is the grand staircase, made entirely of mahogany, and on the platform, or first landing, there is a large bay window, which furnishes ample light to both hall and stairway.

On the second floor are ten large, well lighted chambers, with bath and dressing rooms and spacious closets attached. They are all elaborately finished, as are also the rooms of the first floor, in hard woods of various combinations, worked in beautiful designs. In the mansard story there are several fine chambers, all of them commanding extensive views of San Francisco and its environs, the Bay and its surroundings. The rear portion of this story is occupied by the servants.

California & Taylor Streets, San Francisco

Roun & Taylor, Architects

PLATE 6

Residence of Mr. James C. Flood

 YIELDING precedence to none, this massive mansion stands on California Street, between Mason and Taylor, a monument to wealth. The rectangular shaped main building is a combination of the Doric and Ionic orders. Brownstone steps mount to the front portico. The doors of the front entrance on the California Street side, as well as those at the carriage entrance on Sacramento Street, are magnificent portals of English oak, with hinges and scrollwork of wrought bronze. The front vestibule has a high wainscot of Numidian marble—the floor and arched ceiling are Mosaic. The vestibule doors, also of English oak, give into the antehall, beyond which extends the main entrance, on either side of which is a small room. The hallways are spanned by archways resting upon caryatides, and lighted by a huge ceiling light of opalescent glass directly above the main hall, which is open clear to the ceiling of the second story. Light is also diffused from the triple grand stained glass window in the Sacramento Street side of the building immediately above the first landing of the grand central staircase, constructed of San Domingo mahogany.

On the first floor, by means of sliding doors, all the apartments may be thrown open, making, with the halls, one vast and varied expanse. The frescoes, the floors inlaid in various designs, with many colored woods, and the walls tapestried, frescoed or hung with silken hangings, lend an indescribable air of taste and refinement, while the San Domingo mahogany, richly carved and worked in the style of the Flemish Renaissance, gives a dignity to the woodwork of the halls and stairway. On the first floor, to the right of the antehall, is the reception room, finished in teak and black oak. Opposite is the library, in Carcassian walnut. On the right of the main hall is the drawing room, finished in white and gold. Connecting with the dining room is the ballroom or music room. Opposite is an antehall with breakfast room and the butler's pantry, which is between the two. Beyond are the servants' hallway, entrance and stairways. The servants' hallway has an entrance on Sacramento Street, in connection with the Cushman Street gateway and the carriage drive.

On the second floor all the rooms open out into the main hall or picture gallery, which is lighted by the opalescent ceiling light above. In the tower is the boudoir, finished with ivory and gold, the walls hung with blue silk brocade. Opening from the boudoir is Miss Flood's apartment finished in light bird's-eye maple. At the left of the boudoir is Mrs. Flood's room, finished in mahogany. Beyond, on the Mason Street side, is Mr. Flood's room, in dark oak. On the Mason Street side are also the room of J. C. Flood, Jr., finished in black birch, and the smoking room, in Moorish style, with domed skylight of irridescent glass, in Oriental design. Beyond Miss Flood's room, over the dining room, is an immense guest chamber in walnut. To each chamber are attached rooms for the toilet, dressing and bath. The basement contains the kitchen, laundry, wine cellar and kindred apartments. The servants' portion is isolated from the rest of the house.

California & Mason Streets, San Francisco

Augustus Laver, Architect

PLATE 7

Residence of Mr. Edward W. Hopkins

STANDING on the southeast corner of California and Laguna Streets is this excellent illustration of the modern Gothic style of architecture. The deep gray of the basalt blocks in the basement and second story finds a striking contrast in the red walls, roof and tall chimneys of the second and third. A flight of three steps leads to the platform before the heavy doors of Spanish cedar, which fold back against the sides of the vestibule, paved with colored marbles. The vestibule doors, also of Spanish cedar, are beautifully carved, their upper panels lighted by twelve squares of beveled glass. These doors open directly into the hall, which is nearly square, and lighted by two large windows of stained glass on the east side—one with window seat at foot of staircase, the other at the landing halfway up.

Set in the north wall, at the left of the front entrance, is the hall fireplace of basalt, with hearth set in dark tiles, upon which rest the brass andirons. Above the mantel, and between two windows of stained glass, is the family coat-of-arms, carved in Spanish cedar. All the woodwork of this story is of Spanish cedar, with the exception of a magnificent mahogany mantel in the reception room at the right of the hall. The floors are of oak.

At the end of the hall, directly opposite the front entrance, is the door of the billiard or sitting room, which includes the entire width of the house. This room also communicates with the reception room, and with the dining room in the rear. The latter is a fine apartment, the Spanish cedar showing to particular advantage in the wainscoting, in the mantel with its brass fireplace of *repousse* work, and in the sideboard, buffet and ceiling. A square bow window cuts off the southwest corner of the room. On either side of the fireplace in the mantel are closets, with cathedral window doors. From the east side of the dining room, doors open into the lavatory, rear hall and stairs, and the pantry. The basement contains the kitchen, laundry, wine room and servants' apartments.

In the second story, directly over the front door, is one of the guest chambers, finished in cocobola wood. Over the reception room is a room finished in oak, while opening out of that, on the west side, is the nursery, finished in cherry wood. On the other side of the hall is another guest chamber in walnut. At the south end of the hall a door opens into the principal chamber, with bathroom and dressing room attached—a large, sunny, well lighted apartment, finished in oak, and commanding a view of the Western Addition. On this floor are bathrooms, linen closets, back hall and attic stairs. The third story contains the girls' room, sewing room, trunk room and children's play room. Throughout the house electricity rings bells, carries messages and lights the gas.

Plate 8

Laguna & California Streets, San Francisco
Clinton Day, Architect

Residence of Mr. Samuel G. Murphy

KEEPING very close to requirements of the modernized colonial style, this residence on the south-east corner of Bush and Jones Streets harmonizes in arrangement, finishing and furniture, with the distinctive features of the early American style of architecture.

The front entrance on Bush Street is reached through the gabled porch which leads to the massive doors of the vestibule, the floor of which is inlaid with oak and walnut. The vestibule doors of paneled redwood, with beveled squares of plate glass in the upper sash, open directly in the square entrance hall, floored in oak and walnut, the walls of deep terra-cotta in oil, with a deep frieze in water colors, extending one third from the ceiling, which is frescoed with flowers. An exquisite piece of spindle work and arch, after Moorish design, executed in Port Orford or white cedar, separates the front hall from the back, and screens the staircase from view. At the right of the entrance hall is the reception room, finished in redwood and mahogany, with fireplace set in tiles, and mantel of mahogany and large plate mirror. A square bay window cuts off the northwest corner of the room. Beyond the reception room is the library, also finished in mahogany and redwood, with beautiful west window. Both of these rooms are tinted in the cool French gray on the walls, with frieze and ceiling frescoed.

Beyond the drawing room is the dining room, floored in oak and walnut, with high paneled dado of white cedar; above which is mahogany finished with a frescoed frieze. Here is a genuine colonial fireplace of pressed bricks, with elaborate mantel of old English oak, containing double shelves, cabinets, and set with plate glass mirrors in circular and diamond shape. A square bay window cuts off the southwest corner of the dining room; on the east side of both drawing room and dining room, doors open into the back hall, which also leads to the pantry at the left of the dining room, and through the pantry is reached the basement, where the kitchen, laundry, storerooms and servants' quarters are situated. The grand staircase of white cedar mounts to the hall of the second story. The arrangement of this second story is in accordance with the New York plan, called the "saloon floor" or "saloon plan," and is a new feature in San Francisco architecture. By it two bedrooms may be thrown into one, or remain separate chambers. By this means the second floor may also be converted into an open space. Off each bedroom is an alcove. These alcoves join or face each other, and are connected or separated by sliding doors.

The second floor is finished in Port Orford cedar. Each chamber and the hall has appropriate frescoes and ornamental frieze. The bathroom, also, is on the second floor. The tub is of porcelain two inches thick. The water is supplied from below, and noiselessly fills the tub, which empties itself in the same manner. The third floor, finished in redwood, contains several chambers—notably one fine, large guest chamber, from which, as indeed from nearly all the rooms in the house, may be obtained a comprehensive view of the city. The halls are furnace heated, there is a profusion of art glass ornamentation and there are at least eighteen apartments in the residence.

PLATE 9

Bush & Jones Streets, San Francisco
Newsom & Son Architects

Residence of Mr. L. L. Baker

RISING impressively from its foundation on the northeast corner of Washington and Franklin Streets is another instance of the modern Gothic style of architecture. A flight of granite steps leads to the marble platform before the mahogany entrance doors opening into the tile paved vestibule; the doors of which are also of mahogany. Beyond is the spacious hall extending north and south, finished in mahogany with inlaid floor of oak and walnut. The hall fireplace is set in pressed brick in the north, and has a towering chimneypiece of highly polished mahogany.

On either side of the main entrance is a cloak room. On the left side of the hall is the library, finished in black walnut, with large, square bay window, and window seat on the south side of the room. Each window has an upper panel—of jeweled colored glass—with medallion in the center. In the east side is the fireplace with ornate chimneypiece. Beyond the library is the dining room, finished in black walnut and toa wood. The east side of the room is spanned by a large swell bow window, lighted by six windows, each with an upper panel of stained glass with fruit designs. The mantel and fireplace occupies the central space of the bow, with three windows on each side. On the north side of the dining room a door opens into the butler's pantry.

At the right of the main hall is the music room. Between the music room and the grand staircase, which is further on the right side of the main hall and confronts the dining room doors, is a small hall or annex of the larger one ending at a side entrance. To the left of the hall fireplace is a door leading to the back hall and elevator. At the right of the hall fireplace is the door leading to the *porte cochere* and Franklin Street driveway. Still further east is the billiard room, finished in redwood, with mantel of redwood and Spanish cedar.

The grand staircase, with its massive newel posts of carved black walnut and bronze gas fixtures, its ornamental balustrade of mahogany, which is continued as a railing round the staircase opening in the upper hall, rises to a landing, and then in two lateral branches mounts to the second floor. At the head of the first flight rising from the landing is a mullioned bow window of stained glass. The hall in the second story, which runs east and west, is lighted by an extensive skylight. The suites of rooms on this floor are each preceded by an alcove, the door of which opens directly into the hall. Bath and dressing rooms are connected with each suite. In the third story are several fine chambers and the servants' apartments.

Washington & Franklin Streets, San Francisco

Curlett & Cuthbertson, Architects

PLATE 10

Residence of Mr. Robert Sherwood

HOLDING a commanding position on the brow of California Street Hill, near Jones Street, is this excellent illustration of the Gothic style of architecture as adapted to modern requirements. A wide flight of granite steps leads to the platform before the well sheltered Tudoresque porch and vestibule, with its mahogany paneled dado, its lincrusta walls of red ground and silver fleur-de-lis, ceiling of paneled lincrusta and classic frieze in antique bronze. The vestibule beautiful doors are of polished mahogany, with leaded, jeweled, antique cathedral stained glass.

The main hall is oblong in shape, extending east and west, with large open fireplace on the south side, directly opposite the grand staircase. Upon the main floor is the parlor, or reception room, confronting the entrance, beyond it the large living room, overlooking the southern portion of the city; opening from this the dining room, with circular end on the south side, with a fireplace in its center. All these rooms and the hall are en suite. The western portion of the main floor is devoted to the kitchen, butler's pantry, servants' dining room, rear hall and elevator. The billiard room, fronting on the California Street side, is at the right of the grand staircase. At the right of the billiard room is the rear entrance, and leading to the rear hall. The parlor and living room open out upon a belvedere, or balcony, with a southeastern exposure; from it a flight of steps leads to the garden.

The woodwork on the main floor is executed in mahogany and redwood, the hall and staircase being in the latter. Under the staircase are hat and cloakrooms. With a single wide flight of steps, the grand staircase reaches a platform, with its large window of stained glass in elaborate design. From the platform a double flight, or pair of lateral branches, mount to the hall of the second story, which is carried through up to the third story light, with arcaded gallery on the third floor, affording a *coup d'oeil* of the lower hall and staircase. Upon the second floor are spacious bedrooms, with bathrooms and dressing rooms attached. The woodwork of the second story is principally in white cedar. In the third story are several fine chambers, one particularly noticeable on the east side with balcony prospect. From all the windows of the house is a fine and extensive view of the city. In the basement, which, by reason of the down grade in the rear of Mr. Sherwood's lot, is really another story, are situated the servants' bedrooms, laundry, wine cellar and storerooms. The service is electric.

1123 California Street, San Francisco

Curlett & Cuthbertson, Architects

Plate 11

Residence of Mr. James Cunningham

OCCUPYING a prominent position on the Broadway Street hill, near Pierce Street, this residence stands out against the sky with artistic effect. An easy rise of several steps leads to the platform before the stained oak doors of the front entrance. The vestibule doors, of the same wood, with art glass in floral design, open into the square main hall, which is finished in redwood. The floor is of oak, and the sidewalls are tinted in mahogany red. Sliding doors on the left or west side of the hall open into the library, finished in redwood, with cherrywood mantel and bookcases of the same wood. The walls of peacock blue, harmonize with the fireplace tiles. A large window, with a smaller one on each side, looks out upon Broadway.

Beyond the library is the parlor, finished in redwood and cherry, with a large, swell window on the west side, and large window on the north, which, as well as nearly all the other windows, commands a fine view of the city northward to the water, with "Baldwin Park" on the left of the Bay itself, and Sausalito, the Coast Range, Alcatraz, Angel Island and Black Point. The prospect is full of expectancy, and possibilities never exactly the same. It is a panorama rather than a set view, and from its interesting and changing nature, is particularly restful to weary nerves and tired eyes. Realizing how the beauties of a scene may be marred or altogether lost when regarded through the medium of a small or many-divided sash, the architect has justified his fame for fine window effects by spreading before the eye an unbroken expanse of plate glass, six feet in width and proportionately high.

One sliding door opens from the parlor to the library, another on the right to the hall, and a third into the dining room, whose right-angled north bay window, with window seat, is a feature of the apartment. On the east side of the house, on the first floor, are the side entrance, the back hall and stairs, the flight descending to the basement, which contains the furnace hall, servants' apartments, kitchen, laundry and storerooms.

In the center of the eastern side of the hall is the hall fireplace, with handsomely carved mantel of Spanish cedar. To the right of the fireplace a door leads to the lavatory. At right angles to the front door, the staircase rises on the east side of the main hall, makes one turn, and on the landing thus formed are broad window seats. The window itself, a beautiful one of plate and stained glass, has a southern exposure. Directly over the library is the large principal chamber. The rooms on the north side of the house are the nursery and linen or sewing room. In the northeast corner is a room with the angle spread out in a wide bow window. The upper story contains several fine chambers, a large billiard room and servants' apartments. The service is electric.

PLATE 12

2518 Broadway Street, San Francisco

Clinton Day, Architect

Residence of Mr. David N. Walter

THIS is a particularly attractive residence. Its artistic exterior challenges admiration for its extensive southern exposure, its numerous windows having been so arranged as to make the most of sun and air. The grounds are kept in the highest state of cultivation and are even more spacious than is suggested by the artotype. A wide flight of granite steps leads to the entrance. The double doors open into an octagonal tile-paved vestibule with heavy double doors of richly carved mahogany; the upper sashes being filled with small, square, beveled panes of plate glass. The hall runs east and west and is finished in walnut, with an elegant carved chimneypiece over the hall fireplace, which occupies the center of the northern side of the hall. The mirror is unusually wide, and on each side of the hearth is a square seat. On the right of the hall is the parlor, finished in mahogany, with fireplace and beautiful California onyx mantel in the south wall. The southwest corner expands into a large square window, which adds greatly to the effectiveness of the apartment whose furniture is upholstered with Gobelin embroidery, representing scenes from the fables of La Fontaine.

En suite with the parlor, and also with the dining room beyond, is the library, finished in walnut, with well stocked bookcases. The floor is inlaid with oak and walnut. The dining room is a fine large apartment, finished in antique oak of a rich dark tint and handsome grain. The paneled dado is of medium height. The fireplace, in the east, which forms the principal point of attraction for the eye as it glances through the vista of these three rooms en suite, is set in a beautifully carved chimneypiece, with handsome mirror. At the right of the mantel is the carved sideboard, while on the left is a door opening into the butler's pantry, beyond which are the back hall stairs, kitchen and rear entrance. The lower end of the main hall opens also into the same space; the communication being by means of a door with the upper sash of jewelled art glass.

On the left of the main hall is a spacious apartment with polished floor, designed for the drawing room, but at present used as the music and dancing room. Throughout this first floor the woodwork has been wrought to a high state of polish and beauty; the framework of the doors is particularly admirable for the heavy carvings and massive proportions. Beyond the music room, and on the north side of the hall, rises the grand walnut staircase.

On the second story the principal chamber is over the parlor, and has an elaborate mahogany mantel. Over the music room is another chamber, decidedly unique as to its furniture, which is an antique set of old oak inlaid with applewood. One of the sleeping apartments has a beautiful mantel of California onyx, and a large south low window. There are other bedrooms besides these, each and every one with dressing room attached. Opening from the rear hall are the servants' room, sewing room, linen closet and large tiled-walled bathroom in the rear. The third is fitted up as a miniature theatre with stage, footlights, curtains, and all accessories for dramatic entertainments. On such occasions the tower is used as the greenroom, and the rest of the space, in front of the stage, is the auditorium.

Sacramento & Van Ness Avenue, San Francisco

Schmidt & Shea, Architects

PLATE 13

Residence of Mr. John D. Spreckels

On all that portion of the peninsula known as "The Mission," there is no finer residence than the one on the northwest corner of Howard and Twenty-first Streets. Its grounds are a third of a block in area. A marble walk leads from the sidewalk to the foot of a flight of white marble steps, which rises to a marbled tiled platform before the massive walnut entrance door. The vestibule pavement is artistically tiled, with walnut dado, lincrusta walls and frescoed ceiling. The vestibule doors of walnut and plate glass open into the spacious main hall, extending nearly the length of the house. It is beautifully arched and frescoed, finished in walnut, with walls of lincrusta in dark red, and deep, artistic frieze.

The center of the hall is open clear through to the ceiling of the mansard or third story, with a walnut balustrade around the second floor. The light which streams through the large stained glass skylight is diffused in mellow rays throughout the halls, and as one stands beneath it, the effect is very beautiful. The soft radiance lights up the dark tinted walls, showing the classic figures in the frieze of the upper hall to particular advantage.

At the lower end of the main hall are the staircase and the door, leading to the back hall and stairs; these are spanned by a double arch of walnut. The apartments on the main floor, en suite with each other and the hall, are of ample dimensions, and are separated by heavily paneled, highly polished walnut sliding doors. The first pair on the left open into the reception room, a dark tinted, velvet papered, frescoed apartment with beautiful ebony mantel. Opening beyond this is the library, similarly finished, and still further beyond is the large billiard room, finished in English oak, with dark maroon colored velvet paper and inlaid oak floor. The ceiling is executed in a unique design after a Moresque star pattern in gold raised paper and delicate moldings.

On the right of the main hall is the music room, in white, with beautiful onyx mantel. Beyond is the dining room and then the breakfast room, which opens into a side branch of the main hall. North of the breakfast room, in the following order, are the butler's pantry, the kitchen, the servants' dining room and the storeroom. In the second story are six bed chambers and two bathrooms, also, in the rear, the servants' quarters and linen room. The chambers are severally finished in walnut, Mexican mahogany and cocobola wood, and are provided with spacious closets. The mansard contains several bedrooms and storerooms. In the cellar are the laundry, storerooms, wine room, and iron meat safe, built into the foundation. This charming residence, which was built about two years ago, is noticeable for its well placed windows, artistic fireplaces, beautiful mantels and chandeliers.

Howard & 21st Streets, San Francisco

Charles Geddes, Architect

PLATE 14

Residence of Mr. William T. Coleman

WHAT the early Californians could do in the way of fine residences is indicated by this excellent specimen of the style of architecture which prevailed in the "50's." It stands upon the southwest corner of Taylor and Washington Streets, and was one of the first large houses built upon the hill. Secure in its substantial solidity of brick and stucco, it rests upon an eminence from which the eye may roam over a view embracing the ferries, South San Francisco, the Bay, the shores of Alameda county, North Beach, Sausalito, and even a portion of those classic remains known as Meiggs' Wharf.

The house, built by an old Californian in the day of his prosperity, soon passed from his possession, as the rest of his fortune likewise left him. From that time until it reached its present possessor, W. T. Coleman, who bought it from Judge Hastings, it has successively been the property of several gentlemen, who stamped their own tastes and individuality upon the residence by altering the original structure, or by adding to it, as their fancy or the exigency of the occasion might dictate, until its Italian architecture had undergone several modifications. To its present owner is due the addition of the vestibule in the center of the front portico, from either side of which it may be entered. The vestibule floor is inlaid with colored tiles, and the ceiling is executed in wood. It opens directly into the main hall, running east and west. The walls are paneled, the floor paved with black and white marble tiles, while the ceiling is finely frescoed, as are all the ceilings on this floor. The further end of the hall terminates at the door of the smoking room.

At the right of the hall is the library, finished in oak and walnut, with its north windows opening into a gymnasium, fitted up with all the apparatus and appliances of the athletic science. The library opens into the dining room, in walnut, with breakfast room adjoining. Beyond these rooms is a hall, with kitchen, storerooms and pantries, all in the L. On the left side of the main hall is the spacious drawing room, finished in white, with expansive bow window on the south, and music room at the rear. At the left of the music room extends a large hall, leading to the porte cochere. It also connects with the billiard room, which is finished in oak.

A door opens from the south side of the drawing room into the conservatory, filled with the choicest plants and a luxurious growth of beautiful ferns. A winding staircase leads to the second story, which is devoted to the bed chambers and bathrooms. The addition which contains the vestibule was carried up to this second floor, making a dressing room. The L in the rear of the house is three stories high. A circular staircase also leads to the cupola, from which a comprehensive view may be obtained.

Taylor & Washington Streets, San Francisco

PLATE 15

Residence of Mr. James B. Stetson

FINE residences beautify the upper portion of Van Ness Avenue, and upon the northwest corner of its intersection with Sacramento Street is this impressive building. A flight of white marble steps, flanked by white granite, leads to the platform before the doors of the vestibule, the pavement of which, like the platform, it tessellated in colors. Double doors of black walnut, with large plate glass panels, open into the main hall. The sidewalls are decorated in gold and red. The first room on the left of the hall is the parlor, with an elegant mantel of California onyx, the walls in cafe-au-lait. Extensive mirrors line the black walnut folding doors, both on the parlor and the library side of the main hall.

Beyond the library is the dining room, separated from it by folding doors whose upper panels are etched in glass. The library sidewalls are dark blue, enlivened by gold. The dado is a combination of gold and bronze, to represent Oriental metal work. The ceiling is frescoed in the favorite "sun burst" design, bordered with blue, and flowers. The bookcases of black walnut rise on either side of the door at the north end of the room, which opens into the main hall. All the doors on this floor are of black walnut, heavily paneled, and of great height. The ceiling of the dining room is frescoed in a fruit design, the walls are dark red, and the dado is paneled walnut. The entire southern end of the room is a large bay window, beautifully arched. The floor of this window expanse is set in colored tiles. Another mantel of California onyx is here seen in the western wall of the dining room. The northern end of the room is marked by a unique arrangement of the buffets, in black walnut.

At the right of the dining room mantel a door opens into the butler's pantry, which in its turn opens into the rear hall, with side entrance. Beyond is the kitchen. The main staircase starts from the front hall, and, after reaching half its height, is broken by a platform, from which it reverses its direction and mounts to the second floor. Directly above the landing is the great dome, its center of stained glass, supported by slender Corinthian columns, which rise from the balustrade round the hall on the second floor. The frescoeing is in orange and black, ornamented with gold. The columns harmonize with the coloring of the dome, and the sidewalls are of a neutral tint. The bed chambers are large, spacious and well lighted, with dressing rooms and baths attached. In the mansard are the servants' apartments. The billiard room is in the basement. The residence is heated throughout by a hot water furnace; the service is electric.

Van Ness Avenue & Clay Street, San Francisco

A. C. Macy, Architects

Plate 16

Residence of Mr. Henry L. Tatum

LOOKING off toward the north, with an extensive water prospect, stands this picturesque residence on the southeast corner of Pacific Avenue and Pierce Street. The house is an excellent illustration of the modern Gothic style of architecture, and is exquisitely finished, the interior woodwork having been wrought to a high degree of polish and beauty. Passing beneath the gabled porch, upon the tessellated floor of the vestibule, one is confronted by a pair of massive, heavily-carved, oaken doors, with stained, leaded, antique glass panels, which swing back to give entrance to the oak floored main hall. This is nearly square in dimensions, with fireplace of pressed brick, and pictured tiles bearing scenes from Sir Walter Scott's novels upon their shining surface, upon the east wall of the hall.

Further back, but still on the east, is the staircase of polished redwood and Spanish cedar, executed in spindle work, whose oaken flight mounts by several turns to the second story. A large window of stained glass rises from the first landing and lights both upper and lower halls. The ceiling of the hall is divided into squares by heavy moldings, the whole being constructed of polished redwood. A high, square paneled dado, of the same wood, individualizes the hall, at the further end of which are two bookcases, hung with curtains, in the space of the dado. On the left or west side of the hall is the parlor, floor of oak, finished in redwood and mahogany, the chimneypiece being of the latter. The windows are all great sheets of plate glass. Beyond the parlor is the dining room, finished in prima vera, with high dado in lincrusta. Beyond are the butler's pantry, kitchen and laundry, beside the back hall stairs and side entrance, shut off from the main hall by a door. The basement is unfinished.

Upon the second floor are four spacious bedrooms, the principal chamber being very large and commodious, with dressing rooms attached. Each room is furnished in a wood which corresponds with the woodwork of the chimneypiece. The windows in some instances are fitted with window seats; the walls are delicately tinted. On the third floor are the billiard room and four bedrooms, with the servants' apartments. The house is well supplied with bathrooms, closets, speaking tubes, electric bells and electric lighting of gas. The mantels are very artistic, and the lantern shaped chandeliers in the lower hall are of stained and jeweled glass. The lawn and garden about the residence are very beautiful.

PLATE 17

Pacific Avenue & Pierce Street, San Francisco

Clinton Day, Architect

RESIDENCE OF MR. LELAND STANFORD

ON the next artotype combines the residences of Senator Stanford and Mrs. Mark Hopkins. That of Senator Stanford is one of the most elegant private homes in America, palatial in the magnificent size of its apartments, the richness of its interior finish and the splendor of its luxurious appointments. From its windows may be seen a varied view of land and water, extending from the Coast Range to the Pacific, and from Angel Island southward until the landscape fades away in the hazy distance beyond San Jose. It has an extreme width east and west of 155 feet; a depth of 130 feet. The number of rooms, in this elegant home without enumerating the many apartments of inferior size, is over fifty.

The exterior is imposing; the architecture is in the Italian style, with the bow window as the prevailing feature. The front is adorned with an elaborate portico. The main entrance is into a vestibule finished in French walnut and amaranth, mahogany panels, and the figure of a large dog in the Mosaic pavement. The two doors, opening severally on the porch and into the main hall, are made of almost solid rosewood and mahogany, several inches in thickness. The grand hall is a great apartment of itself, having a depth of 80 feet, a width at either end of 20 feet, and at the center, where it broadens into the rotunda, a diameter of 30 feet. The entrance is flanked with Corinthian columns of red Aberdeen granite. The front section of the hall is relieved by two immense wall mirrors with marble plinths on either side in richly carved frames. The frescoeing is in the richest style of the Florentine.

From the further end of the hall rises the grand staircase, a mass of solid mahogany, relieved by ebony, with balusters in imitation of antique vases and an elaborate and massive newel post. The entire floor of the long hall is laid with encaustic English tiling. The rotunda, octagonal in general design, opens through a circular well twenty-five feet in diameter to the roof. In each corner is a lofty mirror, flanked by double columns of red Scotch granite. Huge sliding doors of mahogany and ebony, with mirrors, open on one side into the library, and on the other into the music room and art gallery. The well opening is defended by a handsome railing. The floor of the hall below the rotunda is made in imitation of brecciated marble, with the signs of the zodiac arranged in a circle.

Just above in the style of the frescoed ceiling are allegorical representations of the days of the week. The first apartment on the Powell Street side of the mansion is the reception room, or the Indian Room. The ceilings are

painted in delicate colors on canvas. The woodwork is ivory finished in cherry. Back of the reception room is the library, the woodwork a combination of rosewood and mahogany. The ceiling is painted on canvas, the frieze is adorned with the portaits of Shakespeare, Humboldt, Agassiz, and J. Fennimore Cooper, while those of Morse, Franklin, Stephenson, and Fulton ornament the central panel. The principal feature of the room is an immense mantelpiece. South of the library and communicating therewith by a large sliding door, is the billiard room, the woodwork of California laurel and rosewood. The ceiling is also painted on canvas.

The southeast corner of the building is the family sitting room, finished in birch, rosewood and toa wood. The ceiling is frescoed in the Renaissance style. The chandeliers are of fine bronze with glass pendants elaborately cut. In the southwest corner is the dining room, with two immense bow windows and an outlook over the southern part of the city and in the direction of Lone Mountain. In the woodwork French and American walnut predominates. The buffet is a magnificent combination of mirrors and marble. The recess of the west window is tile-paved and has a glass fountain. The butler's pantry adjoining is finished in light colored woods in the intermediate Gothic style, and has an electric annunciator, burglar alarm and plate warmer.

North of the dining room, and opening westward from the rotunda, are the art gallery and music room, in neutral tints in the style of Louis XVI. The ceiling is arabesqued; the art apartment is paneled with portraits of artists; the one devoted to music has music trophies and medallion heads of the masters. The large parlor for state occasions is called the Pompeiian room. The ceilings are on canvas, in the style characteristic of the period represented. The woodwork is finished in ivory, after the same school. All the sleeping rooms in the second story are finished in birch, holly, mahogany and maple. The arch of the rotunda is relieved by allegorical paintings. The chambers are designated by the characteristic color of furniture. They are elegantly finished.

Below stairs, the entire floor is finished in polished cedar, and contains the supper room, the servants' rooms, the family breakfast room, other servants' rooms, kitchen, laundry room, drying room, and other store-rooms. The attic forms a succession of high, airy, well lighted rooms. Bathrooms are distributed everywhere from cellar to roof. The supply of mirrors throughout all the rooms is magnificent, arranged to display the costly statuary with which the house is filled. The residence was completed in the early part of 1876.

Residence of Mrs. Mark Hopkins

BY drawing upon English style of architecture for one portion of this mansion, and the Norman for another, there has been attained a result at once rich and majestic. The interior corresponds in scope of design and magnificence of detail with the exterior.

The first room on the first floor proper, on the left of main hall, is the great Moorish room, which looks out upon California Street, with frescoes in which are blended most artistically, varied forms, figures and colors. The parlor on the Mason Street side is frescoed in the Indian style, and is made to harmonize with the French Gothic. The walls are hung with tapestry of embroidered silk. To the west of the parlor is the main conservatory, filled with many fragrant and rare plants. Beyond is a grand salon, or music room, frescoed in the manner in vogue in the middle ages, and finished in solid mahogany, cherry and white. Opposite, the reception room is finished in rosewood, and the frescoeing is after the English Gothic pattern. The impressive library adjoining the reception room is finished entirely in German black walnut.

On the north side of the house is located the dining room, finished in brown weathered English oak, a wood of rare and valuable qualities. In addition to the principal rooms mentioned in this floor is a vestibule and grand hall, whose walls form a picture gallery. Its plan is majestic and colossal. It is eighty-two feet long, twenty-five feet wide and forty-five feet high, reaching nearly to the roof. The cross beams at the top are of carved wood, in unique designs. The panel work throughout the house has been treated in the same way. At the head of the first flight of the broad stairway of English oak is a Gothic arch, on which is painted an allegorical sketch, thirty feet in width, representing "Home." The grand hall is oval in shape, and at the western end at the point where the hall meets the ceiling, is a group representing "Fine Art;" upon the upper part of the ceiling, extending around the entire circuit of the hall, are painted life-size portraits of the great masters of painting, sculpture, architecture and poetry.

The second floor contains the sleeping apartments, which severally are frescoed with the richest designs in white and gold, with symbolic figures in the Queen Anne style, in that of Louis XV., or painted in the tapestry English-Gothic style. The chambers are large, well lighted, with closets, bathrooms, and dressing rooms attached. Altogether there are nearly forty rooms, exclusive of baths and closets, in this princely dwelling. In the basement are the billiard and supper rooms, finished in prima vera wood, and the breakfast room finished in oak and all beautifully frescoed. Adjoining the last room is a sort of conservatory, with glass walls and roof, and a large marble lily tank in the center, encircled by pots of many colored flowers. Closets and storerooms are to be found in convenient and requisite localities. The kitchen, laundry and drying room are large in dimensions and complete in all their appointments. Its view is comprehensive.

MRS. MARK HOPKINS   SENATOR LELAND STANFORD

California & Powell Streets   California & Mason Streets

Wright & Sanders   *Bugby & Sons*

PLATE 18

Residence of Mrs. Theresa Fair

VIEWED from any standpoint, this is a fine residence on the northwest corner of Pine and Jones Streets. A flight of stone steps rises from Pine Street to the front entrance; while from Jones Street the driveway leads to the *porte cochere*. The artotype gives an excellent idea of the mansion. The front doors, with their pictured panels of stained glass, open into the main hall, which is beautifully frescoed, and its sidewalls painted in a Moorish design upon a delicate pink ground. Upon the right of the hall is the reception room, in white, blue and gold; white marble mantel, and tall mirror. A door on the east side of the reception room opens into a small apartment, which is an anteroom for the hall and *porte cochere* on the Jones Street side.

On the left of the main hall is the grand *salon*, a room of magnificent dimensions, the sidewalls also painted in soft tints, the ceiling frescoed by the hand of a master. The one is styled "Love's Offering," the other "Cupids at Play." At the further end of the *salon* hangs Toby Rosenthal's great painting, "The Seminary Alarmed." A great bow window swells out on the western side of the *salon*; a multiplicity of magnificent mirrors flash back the light, rich tints and colorings, and apparently extend the perspective indefinitely. Beyond the parlor is the library, finished in oak, with paneled dado, richly carved mantel, with tiles illustrating scenes from Scott's novels, and super mantel, with bric-a-brac shelves, and cabinets with plate glass mirrors. The ceiling is frescoed in ornate panels, the four corners honored separately with portraits of Dante, Shakespeare, Byron and Longfellow. Passing in front of a tall mirror at the lower end of the main hall, the door of the dining room is reached. This apartment is finished in black walnut, with ornate chimneypiece, high dado, sidewalls, red and gold; ceiling frescoed in floral design. On the north side, doors open into the butler's pantry and into the glass closet. Beyond are the rear hall and stairs, the kitchen, laundry, servants' dining room and storerooms.

The staircase, of carved mahogany balustrade and newel post, starts from the right side of the main hall, and, broken by two wide landings, mounts to the spacious hall of the second story, parallel with the hall below, and lighted by great squares of ground glass. Directly opposite the head of the stairs is the music room. In all, there are nine rooms on this floor—sleeping apartments, boudoirs, a playroom and a study, the billiard room and bathrooms, linen closets and dressing rooms. At the northern end of the hall is a flight of stairs leading to the cupola, with a fine view of South San Francisco. These stairs also lead to the servants' apartments.

PLATE 19

Pine & Jones Streets, San Francisco

Charles W. Kenitzer, Architect

Residence of Mr. M. H. De Young

SURROUNDED by a beautiful lawn and flower garden, at considerable elevation above the Street, this house is one of the most noticeable along the line of California Street residences. The vestibule has a paneled dado of mahogany and frescoes of figures. Its doors of solid mahogany open into the main hall, which runs north and south, with inlaid oaken floor, high mahogany dado, tinted sidewalls and frescoed ceiling. On the right are the double parlors, spanned by an arch, and frescoed with life-size allegorical figures. On the left, the first room is the library; floor inlaid, sidewalls lincrusta with dark maroon colored dado, and deep frieze in Italian style; ceiling executed in conventional design. The mantel is of white marble.

At the south end of the main hall a door opens into the dining room finished in antique oak. The ceiling is of wood, marked off into squares by dependent moldings. The floor is inlaid, the sidewalls are paneled to within a foot of the ceiling. This is in blue with gold ornamentation of heraldic figures, the same blue and gold being continued in a section of an arch from wall to ceiling. The sidewalls are also further enriched with coats of arms richly executed in colors. The sideboard takes up nearly the eastern wall. On the western one is a panel filled with a large piece of tapestry. In the north and south sides of the room are two cathedral paned glass closets. The south end of the room is spanned by a Moorish arch of great beauty, which spans a deep recess, in which is the tall white marble mantel, the open fireplace set in tiles and pressed brick, with a seat on each side of the recess, and stained glass windows flanking the mantel. There are also the butler's pantry, a breakfast room, kitchen, back hall and stairs to the left of the dining room. At the south end of the main hall, on the right, is the principal staircase, and also a descent of a few steps leading to the *porte cochere*.

In the basement are the wine room, storerooms, laundry and servants' room and the Chinese room. The ebony doors are carved into golden flowers, butterflies and scrolls. The windows and recesses are hung with yellow bordered, red curtains. The arches spanning the ceiling are massive specimens of Chinese carving, richly gilt. The floor is covered with matting and rugs. An idol sits cross-legged in his curtained alcove; a round mirror, in a carved frame, is in the center of the south end. The north end is also an alcove, arched with carvings and hung with drapings. Rich specimens of gold embroidery, Chinese paintings and pictured panels adorn the walls. Chinese carved ebony tables and chairs abound, and lanterns hang from the ceiling. The grand staircase is mahogany with landing and window seat. A stained glass window sheds its soft light over both halls. All the chambers open into it. There are the principal chamber, with its two dressing rooms, the guest chambers, the nursery, the sitting room, sewing room—all spacious, well lighted and beautifully frescoed. In the third story are the servants' apartment.

1919 California Street, San Francisco

B. MacDougall & Son, Architects

PLATE 20

Residence of Mr. Charles Josselyn

QUITE as much for its elegant interior as for its picturesque outward appearance does this attractive residence on the southwest corner of Sacramento and Gough Streets deserve consideration. The exterior illustrates the modern Gothic style of architecture, its paneled ornamentation harmonizing with the woodwork within. The entrance doors of Spanish cedar, the upper sashes filled with beveled panes of glass, open into a tile-paved vestibule with paneled walls in wood. Similar doors of the vestibule give entrance into the main hall, a spacious apartment, nearly square, floored with oak and finished in Spanish cedar and redwood, with high paneled dado and wooden ceiling. The hall fireplace cuts off the northwest corner of the hall; the mantel is of gray slate, the chimneypiece of Spanish mahogany, with hooded top and chimney seats. The hall is lighted by two north windows, and also by the stained glass window on the south, which rises from the first landing of the grand staircase to the ceiling of the second floor.

It is possible to throw all the rooms on the ground floor into one large apartment, for all of them connect with each other, and open out into the grand hall. On a line with the entrance are first the reception room and then the parlor, on the Gough Street side. Looking towards California Street is the library, connecting with the parlor. Beyond the library is the grand staircase of Spanish cedar, with sidewalls in Spanish cedar and redwood panels. Between the hall fireplace and the stairs is the dining room, facing the front entrance, and consequently on the west side of the house. It is entirely finished in oak, with richly carved chimneypiece and massive sideboard. On the northern side is a bow window of slight bend with a broad oaken seat. A door on the left opens into the back hall, butler's pantry and cellar stairway which leads to the kitchen, laundry, and to the numerous servants' rooms and storerooms.

The grand staircase, which is a feature of the main hall, breaks into several long landings, and changes its direction more than once to reach the second story. The hall is finished in Port Orford cedar, the sidewalls of a deep terra-cotta tint. The bedrooms and the nursery are all finished with beautiful mantels executed in different woods. The mantels and chimneypieces are particularly noticeable, no two alike, one in every room, executed in oak, cherry, Spanish mahogany, walnut and satinwood—elaborately carved, highly polished, or classic in their simplicity. To each bedroom is attached dressing room with bath. On this floor are also the sewing room and closets innumerable. In the third story are the children's playroom, servants' apartments, trunk room and garret. The view from the upper windows is comprehensive—North and South San Francisco and the Bay being included. All the appointments of the house are perfect. The service is electric.

Gough & Sacramento Streets, San Francisco

Clinton Day, Architect

RESIDENCE OF MR. NATHANIEL P. COLE

MOUNTED upon the northwest corner of Franklin and Sacramento Streets is this stately residence, an exponent of the Mansard roof in domestic architecture. It was one of the first elegant homes erected in this locality, as the advanced stage of the trees shading the sidewalk and the garden shrubbery will testify. It stands in the center of the lot, surrounded by grounds in a high state of cultivation. The front door, reached by a flight of stone steps, opens into the main hall, which extends east and west through the center of the house. It is arched across the middle, the ends of the arch being supported by white Corinthian columns and pilasters. At the lower end of the hall is the main staircase of black walnut. On the left are the spacious double parlors with extensive bow windows, marble mantels with tall mirrors. West of the parlors and entered from them is a large conservatory, filled with a profusion of rare and beautiful plants.

On the right of the main hall are the library and dining room, connecting with each other, finished in black walnut, the dining room having a paneled dado of that wood. Each also has a marble mantel and mirror. Also on this floor are the kitchen, pantry, servants' rooms, closets, back hall and stairs. In the cellar are the laundry, storerooms and wine cellar. The hall of the second floor runs parallel with the one beneath, and into it open the sleeping apartments, five in number, and the bathroom as well.

In the L over the kitchen are other servants' apartments, bath and storerooms. In the third story are the attic, the sewing room, the billiard room and playroom. From the cupola the eye ranges over portions of both North and South San Francisco, the Bay, the outward bound and incoming ships. The house was built some years ago by its owner, who is one of San Francisco's best known and most respected merchants.

Plate 22

Franklin & Sacramento Streets, San Francisco

Wright & Sanders, Architects

Residence of Mr. Frank M. Stone

JUST beyond Twenty-Fourth Street, Howard Street is marked by this most artistic residence. A frescoed vestibule porch, bearing the initials F. M. S. in monogram, extends before the mahogany entrance doors, with art glass. The main hall is square in dimensions, with two large panes of glass at right angles to each other forming its southwest corner, and finished in oak. The floor is inlaid with black walnut and mahogany. The ceiling is of Port Orford cedar, transversed by unbroken lengths of deep redwood moldings. The wainscoting is a high paneled dado. The hall fireplace, set in glazed brick, with its massive mantel of carved oak, comprises over three hundred pieces. Its hooded top is supported upon five short columns. At the back of the portico thus formed are four panels of hammered brass, representing scenes in the departure and return of a crusader. A pair of gas brackets start from each end of this unique chimneypiece.

On the right of the hall and opposite the fireplace is the solid oaken staircase, guarded by two newel posts bearing globes of light. In its flight to the second floor it makes two turns and is broken by two landings. From this landing rises the tall, stained glass window upon whose bright hued surface wanders the storied Marguerite. Opening from the lower hall beyond the fireplace, on the left, is the drawing room, finished in gold with elegant mantel of cocobola, the fireplace in gold and bronze tiling and redwood finishing. The frescoeing is an expression of a sunburst, whose golden rays diverge from the round window at the base of tower, spreading across the ceiling, while into their full glory flies a bright-hued peacock-plumaged bird, the legendary *"wahoo"* of the Japanese, which ever seeks the rising sun. At the lower end of the hall is the dining room, finished in oak, like the hall. Between the dining room and the kitchen, at the north, is a glass closet. Beyond the kitchen, which has every convenience, are the pantry and back entrance. Below are the laundry and a cellar, divided into two parts. A door to the left of the dining room opens from the front hall to the back hall, which also communicates with the parlor and the dining room. These doors are all of solid redwood, the upper portion ornamented with an art glass panel. Here are also the lavatory, side entrance and back stairs.

In the second story the hall is nearly square. Into it open the three sleeping apartments. These are finished in redwood, with the exception of the mantels, which are different. In the principal chamber is one of rich antique mahogany, in the second one of toa wood, and in the third, which looks out upon the loggia in front, one of prima vera. The back hall is shut off from the front. It leads to the servants' apartment, the linen closet, and the bathroom. Encased from view are the stairs leading to the attic. There is also a little round room in the tower.

2818 Howard Street, San Francisco

Seth Babson, Architect

PLATE 23

RESIDENCE OF MR. P. N. LILENTHAL

UPON the southwest corner of Franklin and Clay Streets stands this picturesque residence. As regards its architecture it is an artistic combination of the most striking features of the modern Gothic and the Renaissance styles, the profusion of carved ornamentation being characteristic of the latter. An extremely long flight of steps terminates in an unusually large porch and vestibule, paved and fancy tiles. On the porch are several beautiful porcelain jars filled with plants. The heavy vestibule doors swing back, disclosing the richly paneled double entrance doors, with their jeweled art glass. Beyond them spreads the spacious entrance hall, spanned by an arch supported by corbels, at the point where the staircase hall joins the first one. There are several arches beyond, which add much beauty to the general effect.

The first room to the right is the parlor, with a large California onyx mantel. On the other side of the entrance hall is the library, an apartment embracing the round window in the first story of the tower. Beyond this, and opening into the staircase hall, stretches the dining room, whose magnificent dimensions are augmented by the recessing of the fireplace in the large bay window on the west. The sideboard is also recessed. This apartment is really the feature of the house. It is finished in the Flemish style, the woodwork—with its very high wainscoting, all in black oak—having been brought from Belgium. The furniture throughout the apartment once adorned the interior of some castle "in Flanders." The mantelpiece is massive, and ornamented with panels of hammered brass, the *repousse* designs accompanied by Flemish legends, of which "Oost, west, t'hu is best," being interpreted, means "East and west, home is best."

Beyond the dining room are a breakfast room and pantries, spacious and well lighted. Behind the grand staircase, and hidden from view, are the back stairs and entrance to the kitchen, whose rear is flanked by storerooms. In the basement, of solid masonry, is a large space suitable for a ballroom or assembly, beside storerooms, wine cellar, laundry and furnaces. The direct entrance to the basement is under the front porch.

The grand staircase is very impressive. It makes two turns, and is lighted by a large art glass window. In the second story are five spacious sleeping apartments, each with dressing room attached. There are three bathrooms as well. In the attic are the servants' rooms, with bath. The circular room of the tower has been relegated to the children, and is ornamented with a continued line of pictures on the walls, and adorned by a large Japanese umbrella in the center. A grand and comprehensive view of the city and the Bay may be had from the loggia over the bay window on the right and from the "deck"—the railed platform mounted upon the roof. The residence is supplied with every convenience, including an effective electric service.

Clay & Franklin Streets, San Francisco

Pissis & Moore, Architects

PLATE 24

Residence of Mr. M. A. Hecht

CONSPICUOUS upon the northwest corner of Washington and Octavia Streets is this residence, erected by Mr. J. V. Coleman. but which is now the property of Mr. Hecht. Its new owner has thoroughly renovated the house within and without. It is surrounded by well-kept lawns, and enclosed by an iron fence and granite coping. With its gables and pediments, its round, short tower, its brick foundations, its exterior tall red chimneys, its covered balconies, its windows, accentuated by numerous small squares, it is declared to be the most worthy representative of the Queen Anne style in this city.

Over the porch, at the front entrance, is much ornamental carving, while in the eaves is the legend "A.D. 1885." The embellishment is somewhat unique—produced by squares of mortar, in which are embedded stones and pebbles and bits of abalone shells. The front door is massive, the lower part heavily paneled, the upper with different-sized panes of glass. On the right side of the entrance is a panel of sixty small panes of colored glass. Lions' heads in bronze are the knocker and knobs.

The vestibule opens into the main hall, with its fireplace and stairway also used as a living room. The interior is elegantly furnished; the floors inlaid and highly polished, the walls and ceilings tinted and frescoed most effectively. To the right is the parlor, with swell window and window seat, the mantel ebony, with antique carving and medieval medallion. Beyond is the dining room, with high dado, the ceiling paneled in dark wood, with intersecting moldings. The chandeliers are very artistic and the mantel beautiful. The mantel is particularly large and imposing. Beyond is an elegant little breakfast room. On the left of the hall are the library, conservatory, a study, a wine room, back hall, and stairs to the basement, with kitchen, laundry, furnace room and storerooms.

The main staircase has two branches, which unite at a landing upon which is a long seat and a tall art glass window. In the second story are the sleeping apartments, with dressing rooms attached, also bathrooms and linen closets. The chambers open upon the loggias, and all have a fine view. In the attic are the servants' apartments. Nothing can ever deprive this house of its commanding position in regard to the view, which comprehends the Bay, the Coast Range, Sausalito, Mount Tamalpais, and much of San Francisco.

Washington & Octavia Streets, San Francisco

Bruce Price, New York, Architect

Plate 25

Residence of Mr. John I. Sabin

PICTURESQUE in the extreme, and one of the most unique of all the artotype series, is the house of Mr. John I. Sabin, of the Pacific Bell Telephone Company. It is on the corner of Pierce and Pine Streets. The ideas of Mr. Sabin were successfully carried out by his architect, rendering the result somewhat different from the usual appearance of the houses of today. On either side of the porch, which is protected by a wide, overhanging gable, a long bench rests against the wall of the house. The double doors are wide, the upper panels fitted with small panes of glass in leaded sashes. The entrance is flanked by long, narrow panels, in art glass of floral design.

The main hall is nearly square, finished in redwood, with the wax polish. The hall fireplace cuts off the further right hand corner. The chimneypiece, supported on Corinthian columns, is very effective; the staircase rises from the left. The dado is paneled, with a circle in each square. The sidewalls are terra-cotta, and the ceiling is marked off by deep moldings. On the right is the spacious parlor, with its grand swell window of five double sashes on the Pine Street side. There is another window at the further part of the same wall, also one of rich stained glass. The sidewalls and ceiling are cafe-au-lait in tint, with a narrow blue frieze. The chimneypiece is redwood, with plate mirror. The fireplace is set in light tiles. The chandeliers are hung with crystal pendants.

On the left of the hall is the dining room, finished in similar style as to dado. The ceiling is deep terra-cotta, also the walls. Double windows look out upon Pierce Street. To the left of the dining room is the library or "den," in cafe-au-lait, with chaste mantel; fireplace in pressed brick. A right angled pair of windows light this room. From the dining room a door opens into a passage, leading to the butler's pantry, back hall and stairs. In another direction is the descent to the basement, with the kitchen, laundry, wine room, large pantry, and two servants' rooms and bath. The front staircase makes one turn and then is walled in, or, as it is called, a blind staircase.

The upper hall extends across the back of the house, and is lighted with several windows. There is a linen closet at the further end. To start from this end, one passes through the nurse girl's room, the children's sleeping apartment, then through a dressing room with lavatory, another bedroom for the children, then into the spare bedroom—for all these rooms connect. Over the parlor is the principal chamber, with dressing room, lighted from Pine Street. The mantels are very beautiful, and the tints are soft and harmonious, both in first and second floors, with the carpets, furniture, and elegant portieres. There is an artistic balustrade on the stairs leading to the third story, in which are several rooms—lighted by windows in the gables. The large, front corner room, with dormer windows, is devoted to the children for a playroom. Electric appliances are used throughout the house.

Pierce & Pine Streets, San Francisco

PLATE 26

Residence of Mr. A. N. Drown

LOOKING toward the south, and sweeping a comprehensive view toward the north, stands this picturesque residence on the northeast corner of Jackson and Pierce Streets. It is of the Eastlake order of architecture, with a free Renaissance treatment. Opening from the wide front porch are the double entrance doors of cherry, the vestibule finished in the same, with paneled dado, and floor paved with colored tiling. The heavy vestibule doors, set with jeweled art glass, open into the entrance hall, finished in mahogany. On the right of the entrance hall is the library, finished in black walnut, with fireplace in the north side, chimneypiece of black walnut. On the left of the main hall are the parlor, living room and dining room, en suite, the latter finished in oak. Adjoining is the butler's pantry, with dumb waiter in communication with the kitchen in the basement; in the northeast corner is the breakfast room.

Just beyond the library, on the right of main hall, is the staircase hall, which opens out upon a belvedere or uncovered terrace, from which steps descend to the garden. In connection with the terrace is the covered porch and the side entrance to rear hall, rear stairs and trunk elevator. The grand staircase consists of four flights and three square landings, from one of which rises a rich art glass window, lighting both upper and lower halls.

Upstairs are the sleeping apartments. The principal chamber is over the library, with bathroom, dressing room and closets, over the front door. There are two other chambers on this floor, each with dressing rooms attached. The dimensions of all the rooms in the house are particularly large and spacious. The rear portion of this story is taken up with the sitting room and sewing room, with linen closet between. The view from the oriel windows in the rear is remarkably fine, comprehending the Bay, Coast Range, Sausalito and much of San Francisco. In the attic are the gymnasium, servants' rooms and storerooms. The rear portion of the basement is occupied by the kitchen, laundry, wine cellar and storerooms.

PLATE 27

Jackson & Pierce Streets, San Francisco

Curlett & Cuthbertson, Architects

Residence of Mr. D. E. Allison

STANDING in a prominent position on Broadway Street, between Webster and Fillmore, is this residence with an exterior quite artistic in its ornamentation. The carving over the bay window in the second story is very effective in its design. The stained glass double doors of the vestibule open into the main hall, tinted in pink, and with its staircase in Port Orford cedar. On the right of the front door is a closet. From the left side of the hall are entered the large double parlors, the arch between them supported on white columns. The front parlor has a large bay window, looking out upon Broadway; also on the west an imposing chimneypiece of black walnut, with bric-a-brac shelves. The fireplace is set in black and green tiles. A swell bay window admits the western light to the back parlor. This apartment opens into the back hall, which is separated from the entrance hall by a magnificent glass door.

Opposite the back parlor, on the east side of the house, is a cozy little library. Beyond the back parlor is the dining room, finished in black walnut. The mantel is quite elaborate. The hearth and fireplace are set in white tiles, with rural themes pictured in light brown. This room embraces the northwest corner of the house, with bay window on the north, which overlooks the Bay and all the surrounding scenery, the Golden Gate, the Presidio, Fort Point, Black Point, Sausalito, the Coast Range, Angel Island, and the ever changing water prospect spread out before the eye. On the right is the butler's pantry, leading to the kitchen and rear entrance.

In the basement are the servants' room and the store rooms. Half way up the stairway is a double stained glass window, lighting the halls in both stories. The front apartment is the sitting room, communicating with a bed chamber through double rolling doors, and a dressing room. Over the dining room is the principal apartment, with black marble mantel and fireplace. There are also another back bedroom, plenty of closets, baths and every convenience. The tower over the front door contains a small room, often used as an observatory. The carriage driveway is on the west side.

PLATE 28

2230 Broadway Street, San Francisco

Residence of Mr. George W. Bowers

PACIFIC HEIGHTS is renowned for its beautiful homes. One of the most picturesque in this aesthetic neighborhood is the residence on Jackson Street, between Steiner and Pierce. Beyond the gabled porch is a tile paved vestibule, the double doors on which are of Spanish cedar, heavily paneled, with jeweled art glass in the upper sashes and in the transom. The entrance hall and the main hall beyond are spanned by an arch of redwood at the point of union. The extension is north and south.

In the first story the floors are inlaid with oak. The sidewalls and the ceilings, with the exception of the hall ceiling, which is paneled in redwood, are executed in dark tints to harmonize with the woodwork, which is redwood in the hall and in the dining room; Spanish cedar in the staircase, with dado of the same. The hat stand against the east side of the hall is placed between two art glass windows. The staircase makes one turn, and reaches a square landing, with two window seats and art glass panes in two sides of the square.

On the left is the front parlor, with its great bay window facing on Jackson Street; the fireplace on the west side, set in green tiles, with ornate mantel and chimneypiece of Spanish cedar, with supporting classic columns. Beyond is the library, or back parlor, its fireplace also on the west side of the house, with elegant black walnut mantel and window on either side. Reached by a door from both parlors is a tile-paved conservatory, enclosed in a large bow window. En suite with the parlors is the dining room. It has one west window, besides those on the north end of the room, which, spanned by an arch in spindle work, is occupied by the fireplace, with its rich redwood mantel and mantel top, flanked on either side by a wide window and its window seat. From this portion of the house is obtained a comprehensive view of the Bay, the Coast Range, Tamalpais, Sausalito, Angel Island, the Presidio and Black Point. The elevation in the rear—the hill sloping away from the house—insures the view from never being shut out by any subsequently erected buildings.

On the right or eastern side of the house is the buffet, with the butler's pantry on one side, the kitchen beyond, and a deep china closet on the other. The door opening from the dining room to the hall has within it a remarkably beautiful art glass sash. The north end of the front hall is filled by a cabinet of rare curios. Opposite the door of the back parlor and under the stairs is the lavatory. In the second story the hall also runs north and south. The entire front width of the house is embraced by the principal chamber, which, opening into a dressing room, has communication with the large bedroom on the west. The northwest corner, also the northeast one, are devoted to spacious sleeping apartments, between which are the sewing room, linen closet and bathroom.

PLATE 29

2610 Jackson Street, San Francisco

Percy & Hamilton, Architects

Residence of Mr. William Haas

BEAUTIFUL residences have been erected along Franklin Street, but none finer than this one, near Washington Street. The front entrance is approached by a flight of steps which terminates in a covered porch, before the tile-paved vestibule. The vestibule doors are solid antique oak, heavily paneled, and lighted by beveled crystal. The entrance hall opens directly into the staircase hall, the line of union being spanned by an arch, supported in its center by a column which rises from the first newel post of the staircase. The hall extends along the northern side of the house, is tinted in light terra-cotta, and finished in antique oak. Between it and the rear hall is a jewelled art glass door. The fireplace and chimneypiece, with its hooded mantel top, are on the right of the hall. Beyond rises the main staircase, with its three flights and two landings, at each of which is a tall beautiful art glass window.

The two parlors—the dining room and the main hall are en suite. The front parlor, finished in parti-color woodwork, is delicately tinted in light terra-cotta, with cornice in relief in light chocolate. The southeast corner of the room is expanded into the tower windows, giving a grand effect. On the south side is a beautiful mantel of California onyx with tall mirror. The back parlor, also tinted in terra-cotta, is finished in black walnut. The sliding doors between have tall ground glass panels. The dining room is tinted in light olive and finished in antique oak, with dado. The fireplace is set in the west wall, with colored tiles, and crowned by an ornate chimneypiece. The south end expands into a large square bay window.

On the left of the fireplace a door opens into the library, which is tinted in cafe-au-lait, with black walnut dado. A door from the library, also one from the dining room, open into the spacious butler's pantry. Beyond is the kitchen, communicating with the back porch and yard. The rear of the basement is devoted to the laundry, furnace room, storeroom and wine cellar; the front is finished off for a supper room for balls and receptions.

The second floor contains the sleeping apartments. Besides the principal chamber over the front parlor, with its dressing room and bath and sitting room attached, are three other bedrooms, a large sunny nursery, another bathroom and linen closets. The third story, or "attic," has several large rooms and an unequaled view. An air of comfort and elegance pervades the house; convenience has been consulted; electricity flies at the command of the slightest touch. The gas fixtures present different effects in bronze, hammered copper, and combinations of oxidized silver and brass. The grounds, which are on the south side, are clad in green lawn and decked with flowers.

2007 Franklin Street, San Francisco

Schmidt & Shea, Architects

PLATE 30

Residence of Mr. Willam F. Goad

THIS attractive representative of a solid, substantial order of architecture occupies the northwest corner of Washington and Gough Streets. The front entrance is approached by a flight of wide granite steps, leading to a marble paved porch, whose roof is supported on fluted Corinthian columns. The vestibule is floored in bright-hued tiles, and is hexagonal in shape, with a heavy oak dado and frescoed walls. The heavy oaken vestibule doors, lighted by art glass, open directly into the main hall, which is nearly square, as well as spacious. Its greatest length is from north to south. At the north end, confronting the entrance, is the hall fireplace. The floor is inlaid with oak, the walls are painted terra-cotta in oils, the dado is lincrusta, after the style of pressed Cordovan leather. On the left of the hall is the library, finished in black walnut, with a beautiful mantel and chimneypiece, the fireplace set in legendary tiles.

In the center of the left side of the hall rises the staircase with its landing, from which arises the art glass windows that shed light through both lower and upper halls. Here, also, near the main staircase, is the flight descending to the billiard room below. On the right of the hall massive rolling doors of paneled maple open into the drawing room, with its inlaid floor and mirror which reaches from floor to ceiling. Beyond is the music room, with a magnificent mantel of California onyx. Doors from each of these rooms open into the round room formed by the swell window, so impressive a feature of the plan of construction. It is fitted up as a *causerie*, or secluded nook for conversation. En suite with the music room is the dining room, in the northern side of the house. This room is finished in oak, with dado; floor inlaid, as indeed are all the floors in this first story. The buffet is built into the south side of the room. On either side of it is a door opening into the main hall. In the western side is a richly carved mantel, with its towering chimneypiece and tall mirror. To its left is the smoking room; to its right the butler's spacious pantry.

In the basement are, beside the billiard room, the dining rooms for the children and the servants, two halls, the kitchen laundry, furnace and storerooms, and two servants' apartments. In the second story, the hall is directly over the one below. The principal chamber is over the drawing room. There are several other sleeping apartments, including the guest chamber and the children's bedrooms, to all of which are attached bath and dressing rooms. There is also a large linen closet and sewing room on this floor. On the third story are a large playroom and several chambers. The view from this residence is unsurpassed, and can never be obstructed, owing to the position the house holds on the side hill. Not only from an architectural point of view are the interior arrangements simply perfect, but the elegance of the furniture, the richness of the portieres and the rugs, the dazzling beauty of the mirrors, the elegance of the woodwork, and the harmony of the colors leave nothing to be desired.

PLATE 31

Washington & Gough Streets, San Francisco
Curlett & Cuthbertson, Architects

Residence of Mr. William H. Martin

DECIDEDLY unique is this imposing residence, for, though standing on a corner at the intersection of Franklin and Jackson Streets, its front entrance is toward the south, and faces the side of the adjoining house. A flight of broad granite steps leads to a wide marble platform from which rise white marble slabs to the porch floored with the same. The heavy entrance doors of Spanish mahogany roll back, disclosing a tile-paved vestibule with high paneled dado and frescoed walls. The mahogany vestibule doors, with their jeweled art glass sashes, open into the main hall, beyond which rises the grand staircase from the center of the staircase hall. In the first story, all the rooms have oak floors inlaid with black walnut, the designs for the borders being very artistic. Confronting the entrance in the main hall, which has a paneled dado of curly redwood, is the hall fireplace, set in glazed brick with tiles. The hooded chimneypiece and mantel are of carved maple.

The arrangement of windows is particularly effective throughout the residence, noticeably so in the library on the right, with its swell window on the south and those on the east, on each side of the mantel and fireplace. It is finished in black walnut and communicates with the reception room in the northeast corner of the house, which is also entered from the hall by a door at the right of the fireplace. This parlor has a beautiful onyx mantel in the north wall. On the right of the main hall is the dining room, finished in solid oak, the mantel and chimneypiece, the buffet, and the china and glass closets being heavily carved, and massive in their substantial elegance. A paneled dado is surmounted by an olive tint, the ceiling, cafe au lait. To the right of the fireplace a door opens into a small hall, leading to the breakfast room, in oak, with dado and side wall in different tones of terra-cotta. The small hall also leads to butler's pantry and kitchen, back hall and stairs, and basement stairs. Below are the laundry, storerooms, furnace room, wine cellar, large billiard room and servants' room.

From the first landing of the principal staircase rises a grand art window, which lights both lower and upper halls. In the second story the space is subdivided very much as it is on the first floor. The principal chamber is over the library. There are four sleeping apartments, with dressing rooms attached. There are also a sitting room, linen closets and bath. In the third story are several rooms—the servants' apartments—and in the tower a large playroom. There is electricity throughout the house. The view from the Jackson Street elevation is remarkably fine and comprehensive. The residence belongs to the modern Gothic order of architecture.

2015 Franklin Street, San Francisco

Curlett & Cuthbertson, Architects

PLATE 32

RESIDENCE OF MR. LYMAN C. PARKE

KEEPING pace with the rest of the Western Addition, Gough Street, between Ellis and O'Farrell, here shows as pretty a residence as may be seen in the city. The double doors of walnut, with plate glass sashes, open directly into the main hall, which, like the rest of the house, is finished in walnut and redwood. On its right is the parlor, nearly square, with two windows meeting at right angles in one corner of the room. The lower sash of each is one wide, long sheet of plate glass; the upper pane is somewhat smaller, being bordered by small, square, solar panes of tinted glass. This style of window ornamentation prevails throughout the house. The parlor fireplace is set in colored tiles with mahogany mantel and chimneypiece.

Beyond is the back parlor, also opening into the hall and the dining room. The fireplace is set in glazed brick, with chimneypiece of Spanish cedar. In the dining room the woodwork expresses itself in a dado of square panels. The buffet is recessed in the north with china and glass closets on either side. The fireplace, in the wall between the dining room and back parlor, is set in pictured old gold tiles; the chimneypiece is cherrywood. The dining room opens into the back hall, with its stairs and side entrance. Beyond is a square, well-lighted kitchen, with a French range, closets, pantry and door opening upon the basement flight. Descending to the basement one finds the laundry, storerooms, and many servants' rooms.

The main staircase is of black walnut, and with one turn it rises to the second story. In the lower hall is a lavatory. The hall of the second story runs nearly the length of the house. The principal chamber, embracing the entire front of the house, has a spacious closet, lavatory, fireplace in tessellated tiles, and mahogany chimneypiece with mirror. Its crowning attraction is the round window formed by the projecting tower, which contributes so much to the picturesqueness of the exterior. There is another bedroom communicating with the principal chamber; it has four sunny windows, and opens into the bathroom, in which is the linen closet. Beyond is another bedroom, and at the end of the hall is another large chamber with exceptionally fine view of the city. In the hall are several large closets. The attic contains much available space, besides that devoted to a large billiard room with dormer windows, from which the view is very comprehensive.

PLATE 33

1118 Gough Street, San Francisco

Residence of Mr. Henry E. Bothin

UPON the northeast corner of Jackson Street and Van Ness Avenue has recently been erected an artistic and striking residence. Its exterior presents a unique contrast in colors, and its windows are particularly noticeable. Of the heaviest French plate, they vary in size, and some of them are set with small square panes. About the windows appears some heavy carving in wood, which adds greatly to the artistic effect. The front entrance is reached by a stone flight, a platform and oaken steps, which mount to the gabled porch, the roof of which is supported on carved caryatides. The double entrance doors are of solid oak, and recess themselves into the sides of the vestibule, which is paved with colored tiles. The vestibule doors are also of paneled oak, the upper sashes filled with beveled squares of plate glass. The entrance hall is nearly square, inlaid with maple, the ceiling and heavily paneled dado of oak. The side walls are terra-cotta.

On either side of the front door is a small window. At right angles to the one on the right of the entrance is an oaken bench, extending from the front wall to the hall fireplace, also on the south side of the building. This fireplace is set in colorless brick, with a red hearth. The front of the mantel is of white stone, with leaves in sculptured relief, the letter B standing out in the center. The mantel shelf and chimneypiece are of dark rich wood. On the left of the hall, the first room is formed by a wide, sweeping, round window; the sidewalls are of terra-cotta; the floor, like that of the hall, is inlaid. This room communicates with the reception room beyond, also with inlaid floor, large window on the west. The fireplace, with its mantel and broad chimneypiece of ebony, is in the center of the north side. On the north end of the hall, a door leads into the dining room.

The dining room has an unusually large swell bow window, which embraces the further corner and the west side of the room. With this apartment communicate the butler's pantry and china closets. On the further side of the hall fireplace, on the east, a door leads into another large apartment, the library or sitting room. Beyond this are the back hall, stairs and side entrance. The kitchen and basement stairs are also in this direction. In the basement are the storerooms, laundry, servants' room and heating apparatus.

At the northern end of the main hall, to the right of the dining room door, rises the solid oak staircase with its landing, from which rises a window of rich art glass. On the second floor are the sleeping apartments, bathroom and linen closet. The principal chamber is directly under the tower. The one over the dining room opens out upon a loggia, commanding a fine view of the bay and the surrounding scenery. In the third story there are several gable-windowed apartments besides the tower room. As might be expected, the view, particularly from those on the north, is very fine and comprehensive.

Van Ness Avenue & Jackson Street, San Francisco

Percy & Hamilton, Architects

Plate 34

Residence of Mr. Joseph B. Crockett

ONE of the prettiest houses in San Francisco is this one on California Street, near Laguna. The exterior is picturesque, the olive tint of the woodwork being contrasted agreeably with the bright red colonial chimneys. Sheltered by a porch, the double oaken doors fold back into the vestibule, from which another pair similar to the entrance doors, but with crystal panes in the upper part, open into the oak-floored, square main hall. This is finished in redwood, the sidewalls entirely composed of square panels, the ceiling of the same wood, with intersecting moldings. The staircase, the mantel and the staircase arch, the first and last being executed in the spindle work design, are of carefully selected Spanish cedar. On either side of the hall fireplace, in the west wall, is a window with window seat.

At the right of main entrance is the reception room, also with oaken floor, extending across the front or northern part of the house, with a double square window at right angles with itself, in the northeast corner of the room. The fireplace in the north wall is set in yellow tiles. The mantel and chimneypiece of rich mahogany has a large circular mirror in the center, surrounded by small round ones, creating a very pretty effect. The side walls are tinted in a very light brown, with canary color in the frieze and ceiling.

Opposite the front door is the long, spacious sitting room. An extensive swell window embraces nearly the entire southern end of the apartment, while there is another window looking westward. The fireplace is on the west side, and is surmounted by a carved walnut mantel and elaborate chimneypiece. A large paneled door in redwood gives entrance to the dining room on the left, which is also approached through a door at the lower end of the front hall. The side walls and chimneypiece are of terra-cotta, the mantel of oak, the fireplace set in glazed brick, and flanked by a window on either side. The dining room communicates with the pantry; it opens into the back hall lavatory and stairs. In the basement are the kitchen, laundry, and servants' rooms.

The main staircase makes two turns to reach the hall of the second story, which runs with the length of the house. This floor is finished in redwood. The walls are tinted in delicate colors, the mantels are beautifully executed in polished wood, the windows are numerous, expansive, and in many instances provided with window seats. The principal chamber has a southern exposure, with swell window, walnut mantel, fireplace in fancy tiles, the side walls in olive, the frieze and ceiling in pink. To the left are bathroom and dressing room.

On the northern side are the sewing room and the spacious guest chamber, with circular window and window seat. There is also another large sleeping apartment on this floor and another bathroom. Closets abound. In the third story are the children's playroom toward the south, servants' room, trunk room.

2029 California Street, San Francisco

Clinton Day, Architect

PLATE 35

Residence of Mr. W. Mayo Newhall

ERECTED in the modernized Queen Anne style, this residence stands upon the north side of Post Street, just above Van Ness Avenue. The entrance porch is reached by a flight of steps, broken by a landing. The solid mahogany entrance doors fold back into the tile-paved vestibule. The vestibule doors are paneled with the upper part of the door set in small squares of beveled French plate. The main hall is nearly square, and is paneled from floor to ceiling with Spanish cedar and curly redwood. The ceiling itself is of redwood, barred by transsecting moldings. On the left of the hall, the staircase, with its beautiful balustrade of Spanish cedar, makes one right-angled turn. Over each side of the landing, shedding their light over the hall, are several Dutch windows of white leaded glass, in small panes.

On the right of the hall is the reception room, in white and gold, with ornamental frieze. One corner of the room expands into a wide, square-paned window. Beyond, and also across the further end of the hall, is the large living room. On the east, a large bay window has a unique arrangement of its separate lights. On the left or western side are three square art glass windows set in a wide recess. In the north end of the living room is the large mantel of walnut and bronze relief. The sidewalls are bright terra-cotta, the ceiling a tint of the same hue.

Beyond is the dining room, finished in mahogany. The fireplace and chimneypiece are on the left, or western, side of the room; the elegant buffet is on the north side, and on the east is a swell bay window. The side walls are a delicate shade of turquoise; the ceiling a much lighter tint of blue. A door in the north side of the dining room leads to the butler's pantry and kitchen, also to the back hall, which runs parallel with the west side of the living room and the dining room, opening into the front hall. The doors between the apartments on the first floor are all very wide, and roll out of sight, so that the entire floor may be thrown into one large apartment.

In the basement are the laundry, storerooms and furnace rooms. Throughout the house the service is electric. In the second story the hall extends north and south, and is tinted a pale sage green. The principal chamber, with dressing room attached, is over the reception room, and is tinted in light yellow. There are four other sleeping apartments, each delicately tinted. Beside, there are the bathrooms and linen closet. The third story is divided into another guest chamber, a large playroom and servants' bedrooms. The view from the north extension is very fine.

1206 Post Street, San Francisco

Clinton Day, Architect

PLATE 36

Residence of Dr. R. I. Bowie

I N the artotype series there has appeared no more attractive residence of its size than this one, situated on California Street between Buchanan and Webster. While the exterior of the dwelling certainly is artistic, the interior has been so arranged, finished and furnished as to call forth admiration. Passing under the Gothic porch, one is admitted through the double entrance doors with jeweled art glass sashes, into the square entrance hall. This is finished in terra-cotta side walls and lincrusta dado in old gold.

On the left is the reception room. The woodwork is of redwood, the bookcase of antique oak, the fireplace set in bronze tiling and the mantel of walnut. The side walls are of a sandstone hue, bordered with an ornamental frieze. The ceiling is lighter in hue. To the left is the spacious parlor, which extends north and south. At the latter end is the wide curved window, with cushioned seat and art glass upper lights. The side walls and ceiling are tinted in light chocolate, with frieze in darker shades of the same.

At the north end of the parlor, rolling doors with art glass panels open into the dining room. This apartment has the side walls covered with artistic paper, and the ceiling is tinted to match. The fireplace and chimneypiece, on the west, are decidedly unique. Sunk deep in the center of the chimney is a long, narrow recess, lighted by an art glass window. This feature of the walnut mantel is after an antique Dutch design. On either side of the mantel is a window. From the north end of the dining room a door opens into the butler's pantry, beyond which are the kitchen and the laundry. Both dining room and parlor open into the great square staircase hall, or billiard room, on the east, also approached from the entrance hall. It is finished in terra-cotta, and dado of bronze lincrusta.

Across the southwest corner is the fireplace, with its hooded mahogany mantel. Across the north wall rises the staircase of Spanish cedar, making several right angle turns, from one of which rises a stained glass window. The halls of both second and first story receive light from a large skylight above the staircase. The billiard table is a very fine imported one. Under the staircase is a small dressing room. There are six apartments in the second story, besides the two bathrooms and the linen closet. The house is elegantly furnished, with many rich portieres. From the windows may be seen much of San Francisco, the Coast Range and the cemeteries.

2202 California Street, San Francisco

Pissis & Moore, Architect

PLATE 37

Residence of Mr. C. T. Ryland

JUST within easy walking distance of the San Jose depot is this residence, which does not appear to its full advantage in the artotype; for what enhances the beauty of a country residence is an obstacle to its perfect representation by a photograph. In whatever position the artist might place his camera the large ornamental trees and flowering shrubbery are certain to intervene between the house and the sensitive plate, obscuring the shape and architectural beauties of the former. This was particularly the case in this instance. The residence is large, imposing and with spacious halls, and commodious apartments.

The hall extends through the center of the house. On the right are the large double parlors, with walnut folding doors and marble mantel. From the back parlor, sliding doors on either side of the chimneypiece open into the spacious billiard room, finished in California redwood, and ash floor, with fine large north bay window. Opposite the front door, at the end of the hall, is the door of the dining room, which is finished in walnut and California laurel. The billiard room also opens into the dining room.

On the left of the main hall are the library and the sitting room, with side entrance. In the rear are the kitchen, pantry and china closets, also the back hall and stairs. In the basement are the laundry and storerooms. The hall in the second story is square in dimensions; into it open the chambers. There are also the back hall, servants' apartments, bath and closets. The attic is reached by a flight of stairs rising from the square hall. There are nineteen rooms in the residence, which is one of the most prominent in San Jose.

431 North First Street, San Jose

PLATE 38

Residence of Mr. O. H. Bernhard

LTHOUGH this is but a cottage residence, it is far larger than the exterior would intimate. Situated on Third Street, opposite St. James Park, it is seventy-five feet deep, has ten rooms, exclusive of the kitchen, laundry, pantries and servants' apartments, which are located in the basement, besides the half story used as an attic storeroom. The house itself is quite picturesque. The vestibule porch is set in colored tiles. The front door opens directly into the hall, which makes several right-angled turns, terminating at the door of the principal chamber. Confronting the entrance is the library, a *bijou* apartment, with chaste black marble mantel, and walnut bookcases.

Occupying the front portion of the house is a bedroom, and beyond it is the front parlor, which together with the back parlor, extends along the southern side of the house. In the southwest corner of the front parlor is a charming bay window retreat, the long French windows opening out upon a porch. The mantels are also of black marble. A door from the back parlor opens into the bedchamber at the end of the hall.

Opposite the back parlor door is the dining room, with magnificent black marble mantel, and superb piece of cherry wood. The other finishings are in mahogany. A dumbwaiter furnishes means of communication with the kitchen below. Across the dining room stretches the back hall, into which open the other sleeping apartments. A door on the east side of the dining room opens out upon the back porch. The house is furnished with great taste. The side walls and ceilings are beautifully executed. The richest style of wallpapers have been used with dados and friezes to correspond, their colors harmonizing with the elegant portieres, carpets and decorations. The effect is charming, and a cozy homelike feeling pervades an atmosphere of culture and refinement.

It was built by Dr. W. S. Thorne, one of the most popular physicians of San Jose, but it is now the property of O. H. Bernhard who has recently purchased it from the original owner.

PLATE 39

142 North Third Street, San Jose

Theodore Lenzen, Architect

Residence of Senator C. H. Maddox

WHEN this picture was taken, the entire property, facing on First Street, extending between Empire Avenue to Hobson Street, and comprising an area seven hundred and fifty feet square, had just been transferred to the "Hotel Syndicate." The house itself has since been transported to the Alameda and enlarged. On its original site, the Hotel Vendome is now being erected. The picture has been retained in the artotype series because it represents what was once one of the most prominent residences of San Jose. It was erected at least twenty-five years ago, at a cost of over twenty-five thousand dollars, by Judge Josiah Belden. The trees upon the place were long the pride of San Jose, and, as far as possible, have been preserved from the woodman's axe. Many of them were planted nearly forty years ago, and have attained great size and beauty, noticeably several catalpa trees, English hawthorns, and two immense pepper trees, which grow before the entrance. Some of the oaks are nine feet in diameter, and completely covered with ivy. In one portion of the square is a grove of fig trees, which bear the white fruit—a variety as choice as rare.

Before it entered upon its era of change, the house itself was that modification of the Italian style characteristic of the southern states—nearly square in dimensions, with a covered porch or verandah extending around three sides of the house, in this case the portion to the north being enclosed for a conservatory. The front windows of the upper story reach to the floor of the balustraded roof of the verandah, upon which they open. Still further suggesting the old southern plantation were the number of detached cottages and buildings in the rear, comprising the stables, gardener's lodge, cottage, with laundry and servants' bedrooms; and three tank houses, each over an artesian well, the water from which is renowned in the neighborhood for its purity and softness. The united yield of these wells, it may be mentioned, was twenty thousand gallons daily.

The front entrance and hall are in the center of the house. On the left are the double parlors, with white marble mantels, the walls and ceilings papered in the latest style. On the right of the hall is the library, finished in walnut, with windows opening into the conservatory. On the north side of the library a door opens into the billiard room—its walls of deep maroon velvet paper, with gold and brown dado. At the foot of the front hall is the dining room, partly occupying the western side of the house, communicating with the billiard room on the north, the parlor on the south, and with the back porch; also with the kitchen and pantries beyond. Upstairs are six spacious bedrooms, two bathrooms and many closets. In removing this house from its position of years, an old landmark of San Jose was destroyed. But it is ever the fate of landmarks when they stand in the way of progress—they must go.

549 North First Street, San Jose

PLATE 40

Residence of Mr. Rudolph B. Spence

 YING with San Francisco and Oakland, San Jose has some beautiful residences that may be compared, and not to their detriment, with those in either city. This, one of the most picturesque dwellings in the state, stands upon the Alameda, the great boulevard of San Jose. Its magnificent trees—the mementoes by which were kept green the memory of the early missionary fathers that planted them—were sacrificed to the iconoclastic spirit of the age, disguised as a prudential effort to prevent some accident, which might have taken place in a high wind, for the trees were time-wrenched and decayed; there was danger of their falling with a crash of destruction.

The house stands in the center of the extensive grounds. Before the main entrance, on the east, extends a wide porch. The double entrance doors of heavily paneled Spanish cedar and transom are set with handsome squares of art glass. This door opens into the grand hall, nearly square in dimensions, with a round window embracing the northeastern angle, while the staircase with an art glass window, finished in redwood, mounts in the northwestern corner, while the ceiling is squared off by heavy redwood moldings. The side walls are of a deep terra-cotta tint. The floor is of oak. On the north side, to the right of the entrance, is the fireplace, set in pressed brick, with an elaborate chimneypiece of carved redwood, with columns enclosing the mirrors.

Heavy, rolling doors on the left admit to the spacious parlor, tinted in French gray, and relieved by a frieze and cornice of delicate pink. Across one corner of the room rises an exquisite mantel of California onyx, with towering mirror. The hearth and fireplace are set in slabs of marble with tiles. Beyond the parlor still, on the left of the hall, extends a small hall, leading to the *porte cochere* on the south. Into this hall opens the library, finished in prima vera wood. In the western portion of the residence, directly opposite the front door, is the dining room. Its sidewalls are of deep cardinal, with a dark cafe au lait tint on the ceiling. The buffet, sideboard and chimney-piece are all magnificent specimens of carved mahogany and plate glass mirrors. Directly over the buffet are two small squares of stained glass. The chandelier is unique; suspended by heavy brass links are three massive, highly-polished buffalo horns, from the large end of which rises the gas jet and its accompanying glass globe. Beyond are the pantries, kitchen, hall and stairs. In the basement are the laundry, storerooms and wine cellar.

There are four bedrooms in the second story. The principal chamber is a six-sided apartment over the parlor, with a square window and window seat. It is finished in mahogany, with a richly carved mantel and chimneypiece. The fireplace is set with terra-cotta tiles, relieved by blue ones. The tints are peacock blue and deep mahogany red. To this chamber is attached a dressing room, finished in blue and white. The other sleeping apartments are finished in oak, with blue for the prevailing color, one in black walnut, and the fourth also in oak. In the third story are the servants' apartments. From this altitude there may be obtained a fine view of the surrounding country. The stable is picturesque in its way, its interior finished in red and white wood.

The Alameda, San Jose

Clinton Day, Architect

Plate 41

Residence of Mr. D. J. Spence

FAR out upon the Alameda, San Jose's historic avenue, stands this house, one of the prettiest and most artistic of one-story dwellings—and though architecturally it must be called a cottage, it has a most spacious and well-arranged interior. As will be demonstrated by the artotype, its gables, turret and chimneys catch the eye, charming it by their perfect harmony with the structure, while the covered porch, which extends round the eastern and southern sides of the house, forms a delightful place to sit and enjoy the balmy air, and the blissful perfection of a San Jose day. The front doors—double and heavily carved—are enriched by a pair of stained glass panels. One represents a courtly lady in her bower, listening to her serenading swain on the companion panel, as he sings to the amorous sighing of his lute.

The hall is nearly square, and finished in white and redwood. The first room on the left is the sitting room, and is finished in redwood, with curved bay window in the southeastern corner. The fireplace is set in pictured tiles representing scenes from Scott's Waverly Novels. The chimneypiece is very beautiful. On the right of the hall is the parlor, with ebony mantel, gilt supermantel and mirror. The tiling is in old gold. Beyond the parlor is a spare bedroom in oak, and beyond that the dining room, finished in massive ebony, with the whole north side filled with windows and a glass door, which opens into the garden.

Beyond the dining room are the pantries and kitchen. On the left, beyond the sitting room, is the principal bedchamber, finished in black walnut, with mantel of the same. To this room is attached a dressing room and bath, beyond which is the nursery. These apartments are separated from each other by wide folding doors, which, when rolled back, make the rooms en suite with each other. The hall is divided into front and back portions. In the basement are the laundry and storerooms. In the half story above are the servants' apartments. There is also a large stable on the place. The residence was built about a year ago, and has every convenience and modern improvement.

The Alameda, San Jose

Theodore Lenzen, Architect

PLATE 42

Residence of Mrs. L. J. Watkins

THIS attractive country home stands in the heart of the Bestal Tract, North Fourteenth Street, corner of Mission. The surrounding trees have attained great size and are luxurious. Locust, gums and maples line the sidewalk, while within the enclosure, a decided feature of the garden is four spreading palms, a flowering magnolia, and tall sycamores. On the Watkins property there is a well-grown orchard of two hundred fruit trees in full bearing—the number including fine specimens of the Japanese plums, persimmons, peaches, apples and quinces. Groaning under their profusion of fruit, the quince trees have to be propped up to save the boughs from breaking. The English walnuts produced in this orchard have taken the prize at more than one county fair. There are also over one hundred grapevines in the place.

At a little distance back from the front gate stands the house, facing east, with the porch before the double entrance door; also one on the south side of the house. The wide hall, extending east and west, is finished in white and walnut, with the staircase mounting by the north side. To the left is the spacious front parlor, with black walnut finish and white marble mantel. Wide folding doors open into the back parlor or sitting room, its greatest length extending along the width of the house. A door communicates with the south porch. The western wall of the sitting room is marked by a black marble mantel and two doors. The further one is the entrance to a sleeping apartment, which connects with the bathroom in the rear. The door on the other side of the mantel is that of the dining room, which also connects with a lavatory. These walls and ceiling are tastefully papered.

At the right is a pass closet, with a set of drawers for table linen, which communicates with the kitchen, into which a door further to the right also opens. The kitchen is large and well ventilated, with an unusually commodious, window-lighted pantry adjoining. Across both dining room and kitchen extends the back porch, shaded by a huge pepper tree. One end of the porch terminates at the servants' room.

Upstairs the hall runs parallel with the one below. There is a lavatory in one corner. On this floor are four spacious bedrooms. Two of them are tinted. The largest apartment has both a south and a west window, also a door opening upon the upper porch. There are many closets throughout the house, and fireplaces in the bedchambers. In the rear are the large barn, the artesian well and its tank house. Altogether, the place is a pleasant, picturesque realization of a desirable country home.

809 North Fourteenth Street, San Jose

PLATE 43

Residence of Mrs. Murphy– Colombet

ON the northwest corner of Fifth and Williams Streets this elegant mansion rises impressively from the center of its extensive grounds. It is approached by a stone sidewalk lined with strips of grass and turf. An artistic fence encloses the grounds, which are laid out in the highest style of the landscape gardener's art. Magnolias, palms, and tree ferns, of the tropics, grow side by side with the natives of the northern clime. Roses bloom in abundance, and flowers blossom the whole year round. Stone paved paths cross the vivid lawns and lead to the very pedestals of the marble guardians of the garden. The house itself, painted in two shades of green, harmonizes with its magnificent surroundings.

Before the front entrance is a wide verandah, which extends around the southern side of the building. The double doors, with their upper sashes of glass, open into the main hall, which runs from east to west. It is finished in walnut. The side walls are tinted in cafe-au-lait, with oak leaf frieze; the same tint on the ceiling, set off with a conventional border. At every door hang elegant portieres. On the right is the spacious parlor, with its east and north bay windows, its ornately carved white marble mantel, and large mirror in tall gilt mantel top. Cafe-au-lait tint prevails, with a deep ornamental frieze, and the ceiling frescoed in an elaborate lace design. The chandelier is gorgeous with crystal pendants. From the arch between the two parlors hang richly embroidered portieres of silk plush and lace, with a grapevine in arrasene and tinsel.

The back parlor is a miniature reproduction of the front one, in its effect. From it a door opens into the main hall, also one leads into the billiard room, which is finished in oak, with marble mantel, and communicates directly with the rear porch. A door at the end of the main hall does the same. On the left side of the hall, the first room is the sitting room, shaded by the front verandah. It also partakes of the prevailing tint—cafe-au-lait. It is graced by a marble mantel and mirror, and a crystal chandelier. Beyond is the library, a massive arch of walnut, supported on two columns, marking the opening between the two apartments. The library ceiling is frescoed with flowers. Last of all is the dining room, entered also from the south verandah. Here the side walls are in terra-cotta, with a flower-decked frieze; the ceiling bordered with set design. The marble mantel is surmounted by a very elegant superstructure of mirrors, recesses and bric-a-brac niches. Beyond the dining room are the kitchen, pantries, back stairs and servants' dining room. In the basement are the laundry, and wine cellar.

In the second story, reached by a walnut staircase with paneled dado, are several spacious bedrooms and two bathrooms. A second flight of stairs leads to the attic in which are the servants' apartments and bath. The conservatory is filled with the rarest exotics, while the windmill, tank house, gardener's lodge, barn and stables are in keeping with their artistic surroundings.

Fifth & William Streets, San Jose

Plate 44

Residence of Mr. Samuel T. Alexander

AN excellent exponent of the Queen Anne order is seen in this house, on the northeast corner of Sixteenth and Filbert Streets. A high, wide flight of steps, broken by a broad landing, rises to the covered front porch on the south side of the house. The vestibule is paved in colored tiles. The double doors, heavily paneled, and with long glass sashes, open into the entrance hall, which leads to the square stair hall, the point of meeting being spanned by an arch of Oregon maple. The doors are all of this wood. The ceiling is transversed by deep moldings, and the high dado in the halls and the staircase is paneled by crossbars of the same, the squares being fitted with lincrusta, with the effect of pressed leather. The sidewalls and the ceilings are tinted in very light green. The floor is of ash. The staircase upon the west side of the hall makes five turns, with four landings. There is a broad seat across the first landing. A large stained glass window sheds its mellowed light over the two halls. The hall fireplace is set in pressed brick, ornamented with tiles. The mantel and grand chimneypiece are made of the finest Oregon maple.

On the left of the entrance hall is the reception room. Beyond it, in the left or main hall, rises the staircase; beyond that a door opens into the back hall. On the south side of the square main hall is the entrance to the front parlor or drawing room. Here are a curved south bay window, a tall walnut mantel rising above the tiled fireplace on the west, a small round window in the base of the tower on the east, and on the north the wide rolling doors, beyond which stretches the back parlor or sitting room, also entered from the hall and the dining room. It is finished the same as the front parlor, in light gray tone, with walnut mantel on the north, and a very large square bay window looking out upon Filbert Street.

At the right of the hall fireplace is the door of the spacious dining room, finished similarly to the hall. In the northeast corner of the room are two windows at right angles, each one a magnificent expanse of plate glass. Above each are two squares of art glass. A very handsome buffet is built into the rear wall. At its left is the china closet. In the western side of the room is the fireplace, in pressed brick, banded by white slabs. Cut into the one crossing the upper part is the Hawaiian salutation *"Aloha, nui,"* or "Love be unto you." Near the fireplace a door leads to the back hall stairs, kitchen and side entrance. The laundry, storerooms and furnace are in the basement. Besides the bathrooms, there are five spacious chambers, with large closets and drawing rooms. The attic contains four rooms of no small dimensions.

PLATE 45

Sixteenth & Filbert Streets, Oakland

Clinton Day, Architect

Residence of Mr. Henry Wadsworth

ONSPICUOUS among the beautiful homes which line Alice Street, Oakland, is this residence. Its architecture is a modern treatment of the Queen Anne order, and a glance at the artotype will show that its exterior is more than ordinarily picturesque, raising expectations as to the interior which are amply justified. A wide covered porch spreads before the vestibule in antique oak. The vestibule doors are heavy, with art glass panels and transom of the same design. The main hall is impressive from its high paneled dado and complete finish in antique oak. The upper sidewalls are tinted in terra-cotta, the ceiling of appropriately elegant redwood, barred into squares by intersecting carved molding.

The arrangement of the staircase is unique. At the right of the front entrance the adjoining corner swells into a wide curve. This is all absorbed by the first landing of the flight, and possesses a broad window seat in oak. The staircase consequently is upon the right side of the house. That portion of space devoted to it is spanned by an arch supported on columns of solid oak. In this alcove are the hall fireplace with its pressed bricks and band of fancy tiling, a chimney seat and a pointed window under the second flight of the stairs from the first landing. Near the second is a tall art glass window, lighting the upper hall, and also the lower one. Beyond, with a small window, is a reception room in a light gray tone.

On the opposite side of the hall are the two parlors, finished in redwood. The first has a swell window, sidewalls in light terra-cotta, the frieze and ceiling in cream tint, also a cherry wood chimneypiece, hearth set in tiles of a conventional design. Quite near the fireplace a door opens into a sunny little supplement of a room, a cozy nook for an hour's fancy work or novel reading. The second parlor, or billiard room, is a reproduction of the first as to detail of tints and wood. At the end of the hall is the dining room, with a high dado of terra-cotta lincrusta, the rest of the sidewall being of an olive tint, and the ceiling in cream. The floor is of oak.

Another door at the end of the hall opens into the rear hall, back stairs and side entrance. Here are doors leading to the kitchen, pantries, basement stairs and lavatory. In the basement are the laundry and storerooms. Six apartments take in the second story, some with dressing rooms attached. The number of closets in this house is unusually large, there being at least twenty-five. The principal chamber, over the front parlor, has a large square bow window, fireplace and cherrywood chimneypiece. Several of the apartments are en suite. The attic contains two finished rooms, besides trunk room, and considerable space not yet utilized. Throughout the house the service is electric.

PLATE 46

1347 Alice Street, Oakland

Clinton Day, Architect

Residence of Mr. Henry Griffin

HARDLY a stone's throw from the terminus of the narrow gauge railroad, stands this picturesque residence on Harrison Street. Its exterior is particularly pleasing, the architecture being a combination of both the Elizabethan and Queen Anne styles. The fancy shingled sides of the second story, the wide brick chimney with its light colored ornamental tiles, the gables and light iron railing along the room, cannot fail to attract and please the eye. The entrance is very effective. A wide gabled porch, with fancy gas lantern in the center, approaches the heavy mahogany double doors.

The main hall, including the space occupied by the staircase, is nearly square. It, as is all the rest of the house, is finished in black walnut. The stairs rise on the left side of the hall, starting quite near the front door. The hall window is at the foot of the stairs. The newel post is a very handsome piece of black walnut, and is surmounted by a triple branching light. On the right is the spacious parlor, with an elegant mahogany mantel and chimneypiece, with large mirror. The fireplace and hearth are set in fancy dark olive-hued tiles. The front bay window, with its three divisions, is noticeable for the great size of its square center pane. Beyond the parlor is the sunny library, with a large paned swell bay window, with art glass ornamentation.

From the library, on the further side, a door opens into a large square bedroom, with a dressing room and bath attached. From the library on the left, also from the lower end of the front hall, communication is had with the dining room, where, on the side opposite the door leading into the front hall, are doors opening into the butler's pantry and kitchen, beyond which are the back hall and stairs, also the side entrance.

Upstairs the hall runs the entire length of the house, the disposition of space following that of the lower story as to size and position of rooms. There are five large chambers, besides bathroom and linen closets, all well lighted by spacious windows. The upper portion of the house, the attic, has been arranged for a storage and lumber room. In the basement are the laundry, servants' apartments and storerooms. The house has been planned with a view to comfort and convenience. There is electricity throughout the house, and a prompt acting burglar alarm. The sidewalk is of patent stone, and the garden is under cultivation. The house was built about two years ago.

1204 Harrison Street, Oakland

Plate 47

RESIDENCE OF Ex-GOVERNOR GEORGE C. PERKINS

NOT more than five minutes walk from the Adeline Street Station, is this residence, situated in the center of a large square of land on the corner of Adeline and Tenth Streets. A wide spreading lawn stretches before the front entrance, and is bounded by a well graveled path—entered from the two front corners of the lot. Besides the lawns are the garden, a large barn and stable, croquet ground, a poultry yard, venerable oaks and vine clad eucalypti. The house itself, which was built by Dr. R. E. Cole, is a substantial, square roomed edifice.

Its front porch, with balcony supported on columns, leads to the main entrance, with its double doors opening into the square vestibule. The vestibule doors of walnut, with ground glass panels, open into the main hall. On the left of the hall are the two parlors, spanned by an arch resting on columns. A white marble mantel is at the end of the back parlor. One side of this parlor is expanded into a spacious bay window. On the right of the hall is the library, with white marble mantel and well filled walnut bookcases and its cabinet of mineralogical specimens. Beyond is the dining room, communicating with the back hall, and butler's pantry and kitchen.

A large window in the western wall catches the last rays of the sun. The main staircase of black walnut makes several turns and reaches the large square hall of the second story, which, as does the hall below, communicates with the back hall and stairs. There are seven bed chambers on this floor, besides the bathroom and linen closets. In the attic there are several fine apartments.

On the west side of the house is the side entrance opening out upon a long covered porch. The rooms are all spacious, well lighted, sunny apartments. Throughout the house are scattered a profusion of valuable oil paintings by the best artists of the day, and a varied collection of bric-a-brac. In the hall stands a chiming clock, in a tall, carved oaken case, and the parlor is graced by marble forms of statuary. Taste, intelligence and wealth combine to make a home of comfort, elegance and convenience.

Adeline & Tenth Streets, Oakland

MacDougall & Marquis, Architects

PLATE 48

RESIDENCE OF MR. JOHN M. BUFFINGTON

YEARS ago Oak Street was known chiefly by the fact that at its intersection with Seventh Street, there was a railroad station, and that several pioneer residents of Oakland had built their homes in the midst of grounds which sloped down to the water's edge. But within the past decade there have been great improvements in this locality. Numerous fine residences have been built in the latest and most artistic style, and are surrounded by blooming gardens and grassy lawns. One of the prettiest of these recently erected homes is on the lower corner of Oak and Tenth Streets. It belongs to that order of architecture, in which the Gothic gable plays an important part. The house was built several years ago, consequently the grassy sidewalks and garden are in a fine state of cultivation. A iron fence, rising from a brick foundation, encloses the grounds.

The house itself is picturesque, this effect being heightened by the parti-colored and ornamented exterior. The basement portion is of a dark green. Above that is a band of dark terra-cotta color, which is repeated in the window casings. The first story is dark red, then a bank of olive. Above that, in fancy shingles, is the second story, in light green. The gables are ornamented with disks of contrasting colors, while the small square panes of glass in the upper sash of each window give a Queen Anne aspect to the house.

The front porch is well protected by its arched roof. A pair of double doors, with art glass sashes, open directly into the square hall. The staircase is not visible. On the right is the parlor, a very pretty room, handsomely furnished. On the left is the library, which has one corner enlarged by the projecting square bay window, with art glass panes, medallions in the center. Beyond the library is the sitting room. The dining room has a large bay window. Beyond are the kitchen, pantries, side entrance and basement stairs. The house is furnace heated and the service is electric. Throughout the house the mantels and pretty gas fixtures. In the second story are the sleeping apartments, closets, bathroom and servants' bedroom. The stable is in the rear with driveway on Tenth Street.

Oak & Seventh Streets, Oakland

W. G. Matthews, Architect

PLATE 49

Residence of Mr. Wallace Everson

WITH well extensive grounds, and artistic interior, on the southwest corner of Filbert and Sixteenth Streets, stands one of the most attractive houses in Oakland. It is built upon quite an eminence, which slopes down in grassy lawn toward the sidewalk. The house may be said to represent the modernized Gothic style of architecture with its gables and covered porches. A broad flight of steps mounts through the sloping lawn to a broad landing, from which another flight leads to the double doored entrance, with the pavement set in colored tiles. The stained glass transom over the entrance is particularly wide.

The main hall of the house runs east and west, and into it open, by large folding doors, the principal apartments of the first floor. The finish throughout is toa wood. The sidewalls and ceilings are tinted very delicately. On the right is the spacious parlor, with elaborate mantel. The eastern end is expanded into a large bow window, and there is a northern outlook as well. On the right of the hall is the library, with east windows; and the fireplace and mantel on the south. Beyond the library is the music room, also communicating with the main hall. The staircase, executed in spindle work design, makes several turns at its landings before it reaches the second floor. From one of these rises a double stained glass window, which gives light to both halls.

At the western end of the front hall a door opens into the side hall, which leads directly into the dining room, a long, wide apartment, with a grand expansion at the south end, which forms a very large bow window. Several west windows look out upon a lawn. On the north is the buffet, with the entrance from the side hall on one flank and the pass closet on the other. In the side hall are the rear stairs, side entrance and a door opening into the kitchen. In the basement are the laundry, storeroom, furnace room and wine cellar.

The sleeping apartments are on the second floor. The principal chamber is over the parlor, and communicates with the nursery over the library. Over the music room is another bedroom. The sewing room is in the southwest corner. There are three other bedrooms, two with a western exposure, the other facing the north. On this floor is also the bathroom and the linen closet. The large attic is fitted up for a playroom. The stable is on the southwestern portion of the grounds.

Plate 50

Filbert & Sixteenth Streets, Oakland

GLOSSARY

BALUSTRADE
A row of small columns or pilasters joined by a rail, serving as an enclosure for balconies and staircases, or used merely as an ornament.

BIJOU APARTMENT
A small, heavily decorated room, usually with a singular motif.

BRIC-A-BRAC
A collection of objects having a certain interest or value from their rarity or antiquity.

CARYATIDES
Statues of standing robed women used architecturally as support or decorative columns.

CAUSERIE
A small secluded nook used for literary conversation.

COCOBOLA
An exotic hardwood used in fine woodworking.

COUP d'OEUIL
(Coup d'Oeil is correct spelling) Glance of the eye; a comprehensive or rapid view.

CUPOLA
The round top of a dome or any structure. A spherical vault on the top of an edifice.

DADO
That part of a pedestal between the base and the cornice. The finishing of the lower part of the walls in rooms, made to represent a wide, continuous pedestal.

ENCAUSTIC
Painted surfaces fixed by heat, as on fired and glazed tiles. Often used in Victorian interiors as a substitute for marble.

EN SUITE
Refers to a group or series of rooms that open into one another.

FRESCO
A method of painting on walls with pigments on fresh plaster, or on a wall laid with mortar not yet dry.

FRIEZE
Originally, that part of the entablature of a column between the architrave and cornice. A panel enriched with figures or other ornaments. In Victorian architectural context, almost any decorated horizontal panel above eye level.

INGLENOOK
A secluded corner or recess, a retreat, often next to a fireplace.

JEWELED GLASS
Stained or colored glass used in windows, with faceted glass "jewels" incorporated in the design.

LINCRUSTA-WALTON
Name commonly given to wall-covering material invented by Frederick Walton in 1877. It was a moderately-priced flexible, waterproof material similar to linoleum that was usually embossed with repeat designs. Applied to walls or dado surfaces, it could be painted to resemble carved wood, embossed metal, leather or tiles.

MANSARD
Francois Mansard, French architect (d.1666). His name was applied to a roof of two slopes, the lower being steeper than the upper slope.

NEWEL POST
The post above which a winding staircase circles, or the main or secondary posts of a straight staircase.

PORT ORFORD
A nineteenth-century lumber port on the Oregon Coast. Name given to White Cedar from the region.

PORTE COCHERE
A porch fronted by columns and large enough for horse and coach, so that people alighting from the coach are protected.

PORTIERES
Heavy drapes, often hung between rooms.

PRIMA VERA
An exotic hardwood used for fine woodworking.

REPOUSSE
A pattern formed in relief.

SWELL WINDOW
Bay window with curved glass.

TRUNK ROOM
A room dedicated to the storage of steamer trunks and other paraphernalia used for travel.

WAINSCOT
A wooden lining or boarding of the walls of rooms, usually made of panels.

"St. Francis and St. Benedight,
Bless this house from wicked wight,
From the nightmare and the Goblin
That is hight Good Fellow Robin.
Keep it from all evil spirits,
Fairies, weasels, bats, and ferrets
From curfew time to the next prime."

—William Cartwright
A House Blessing, 1651